SO YOU THINK YOU'RE A DUKE BLUE DEVILS BASKETBALL FAN?

STARS, STATS, RECORDS, AND MEMORIES FOR TRUE DIEHARDS

JIM SUMNER

SPORTS
PUBLISHING

Visit our website at www.sportspubbooks.com.

10 9 8 7 6 5 4 3 2 1

Library of Congress Cataloging-in-Publication Data is available on file.

Cover design by Tom Lau
Cover photo credit: AP Images

ISBN: 978-1-61321-971-3
Ebook ISBN: 978-1-61321-978-2

Printed in the United States of America

Contents

Introduction

Basketball is one of the few sports that was actually invented. James Naismith came up with it back in 1891 as a way to find something for his students to do at the YMCA Training School in Springfield, Massachusetts. The New England winters were too cold for outside activities like baseball, football, or soccer, and indoor substitutes like rope jumping or calisthenics were met with equal parts scorn and boredom.

Naismith had a winner, a participant sport that didn't require a lot of room or equipment, a game that blended teamwork and individuality.

It didn't take long for basketball to spread. Colleges and universities were playing the game within a few years. It spread into the South by the first decade of the 20th century.

As the rules changed and became standardized, the game also sped up and players became more skilled. Fans and media paid increased attention. The National Invitation Tournament started in 1938, the NCAA championships the following season.

Fast forward to 2016, and the NCAA has 351 teams playing men's basketball just in Division I, the highest classification, with hundreds more in lower classifications.

That's a lot of basketball, a lot of games, a lot of coaches, a lot of players, and a lot of championships. It's a lot to digest.

But that's also a long time for some hierarchies to be established. The broad consensus is that six colleges have distanced themselves from the field in historical terms. In alphabetical order, they are Duke, Indiana, Kansas, Kentucky, North Carolina, and UCLA.

This sextet has won 37 of the 77 NCAA Division I titles, and each team has advanced to a minimum of one Final Four in at least five different decades.

Five of these six schools are state-supported schools with large student bodies that translate into large and nearby fan bases, expansive facilities, and all the other benefits that come with that territory.

Sustaining dominance is always difficult. But Duke has really defied the odds. Duke is the outlier. Duke is an academically-elite, private school with barely 6,000 undergraduate students, students who come from all over the world.

With the University of North Carolina located less than 10 miles away, Duke likely isn't even the most popular team in its home city of Durham, North Carolina. Duke plays its home games in a facility that opened before the United States entered World War II and reminds many first-time visitors of a high school gym.

Yet, competing in arguably the nation's most competitive conference, Duke has won, won big, won consistently, over a span of time that exceeds a century. Duke became the fourth school to win 2,000 games and ranks near or at the top in NCAA titles, NCAA Tournament wins, Final Fours, poll rankings, and pretty much any other metric one can think of.

Nine different Blue Devils have won National Player of the Year awards in 11 seasons. Sixty-five former Duke players have played in the NBA and/or ABA, and more former Duke players have been selected in the NBA lottery than those from any other school. Duke has never had a losing decade and has never had more than three consecutive losing seasons (and that was in the 1920s).

And that aging gym? It's become college basketball's most iconic on-campus facility, largely because of the rabid and creative support of that tiny student body.

Speaking of icons, there's Mike Krzyzewski, Coach K, the man who took over at Duke in March 1980 as a virtual unknown and hung around long enough to win more games than any other coach in men's Division I history.

Krzyzewski took a program that had been performing at a high level for decades, brought it to a higher level, and then took it higher still.

In the pages that follow, I break down this big block of history and explore the men, the rivalries, the games, the venues, and the competitions that have made Duke basketball special.

1

SLAM DUNK LEVEL

1. In which league does Duke play? *Answer on page 3.*
2. Where does Duke play its home games? *Answer on page 7.*
3. Duke's athletic teams play under what nickname? *Answer on page 11.*
4. What is the nickname of Duke's student fans? *Answer on page 11.*
5. Who is Coach K? *Answer on page 14.*
6. Who is Duke's biggest rival? *Answer on page 21.*
7. Which Duke player is the leading scorer in men's NCAA Tournament history? *Answer on page 23.*
8. Who is the leading scorer in Duke history? *Answer on page 31.*
9. Which Duke player holds the NCAA career record in assists? *Answer on page 36.*
10. What was the Dixie Classic? *Answer on page 39.*
11. Which Duke player was named National Defensive Player of the Year three times? *Answer on page 41.*
12. Which Duke basketball player is the son of a four-time NFL All-Star? *Answer on page 42.*
13. For whom was Duke's iconic basketball facility named? *Answer on page 46.*

14. What is the only college team to have two national players of the year in the same season? *Answer on page 48.*

15. Who is "The Landlord"? *Answer on page 52.*

16. What Duke team was ranked No. 1 in the AP poll every week of the season? *Answer on page 53.*

17. What Duke team went from the cellar to the penthouse in one season? *Answer on page 59.*

18. Who are the three brothers who all played for Duke teams that won the NCAA title? *Answer on page 64.*

19. Who was the first Duke freshman to be voted first-team All-ACC? *Answer on page 67.*

20. Duke's first Final Four and first ACC Player of the Year were in the same year. What was the year and who was the player? *Answer on page 69.*

21. What Duke player scored a career-high 36 points after a two-month injury absence? *Answer on page 74.*

22. Who was the first freshman to be named ACC Player of the Year? *Answer on page 76.*

23. Who was Duke's first McDonald's All-American? *Answer on page 78.*

24. Who was the first freshman to lead Duke in scoring and rebounding? *Answer on page 81.*

25. What is the "Miracle Minute"? *Answer on page 82.*

26. What was the first team to have four first-round NBA draft picks? *Answer on page 85.*

27. Which Duke team was called "alarmingly un-athletic" by a prominent ESPN analyst on live TV? *Answer on page 85.*

SLAM DUNK – ANSWERS

1. The Atlantic Coast Conference. Duke was a charter member of the ACC in 1953 and has never considered leaving that circuit, which has had anywhere from seven to 15 members.

The ACC has been considered one of the best basketball conferences in the nation since its inception. But the ACC was actually founded as a football conference. College football underwent a major expansion after World War II, as the GI Bill fueled an explosive expansion of college campuses, while improved technology spread the sport's popularity.

It all began with a rift that existed in the Southern Conference. Duke was one of a number of conference schools that wanted to play big-time college football in the years immediately following World War II.

Smaller Southern Conference schools decried what they considered an over-emphasis on the sport and in turn demanded a lower profile for football.

The small schools outnumbered the football schools. The Southern Conference even banned schools within the conference from playing in bowl games. Clemson and Maryland defied the ban in 1951 and were suspended from conference play the following season.

The football schools broke away in May 1953, meeting in Greensboro, North Carolina, which has remained home to the league's headquarters. The founding members were Clemson, Duke, Maryland, North Carolina, North Carolina State, South

Carolina, and Wake Forest. Virginia joined over the summer, creating a geographically compact, eight-team circuit.

It didn't take long for the ACC to make its mark on the hardwood.

The Southern Conference had 17 teams in 1952-53, playing anywhere from 11 to 21 conference games. Some teams played each other twice, others didn't play at all.

The only way to determine a conference champion was to have a postseason tournament, usually consisting of eight teams.

The ACC inherited this format for its first season, a season with an unbalanced schedule; late-arrival Virginia only played five ACC games that first season.

But the ACC decided to continue the format, with all eight teams playing a single-elimination tournament to decide the official conference champion and the league's automatic bid to the NCAA Tournament.

None of the other big conferences determined their champion this way, preferring the grind of a regular season.

The ACC did occasionally pay a competitive price as a result of this format. Some of the best teams in the league's first two decades saw their seasons end prematurely due to a bad night. South Carolina went 14-0 in the 1970 ACC regular season. But their best player suffered a sprained ankle in the ACC Tournament and they were upset in the finals, ending their season at 25-3.

But on balance, the ACC Tournament was a huge advantage. Not only did it put the new league firmly on the map, but also it generated a tsunami of enthusiasm, especially in the state of North Carolina, home to half of the league's eight teams and host of every ACC Tournament until 1976.

North Carolina State's Everett Case came to NC State in 1946 and captured nine Southern or ACC Conference tournaments in his first 10 seasons. Case elevated the sport in the mid-Atlantic but was never able to go all the way. The first ACC team to capture the national title was North Carolina, which went 32-0 in 1957.

The 1957 finals were held in Kansas City. After North Carolina captured the East Regional, Greensboro business-man Castleman D. Chesley put together an impromptu, three-station network to televise North Carolina's games back to North Carolina.

It was a huge gamble for Chesley and it paid off in a big way. Families with televisions opened their homes to neighbors, while stores selling TVs stayed open well past their normal closing times.

North Carolina defeated Wilt Chamberlain and Kansas 54-53 in three overtimes and the ACC never looked back. The conference contracted with Chesley for a full season of conference basketball and beginning in 1958 the ACC game of the week became a Saturday staple.

No other conference had anything like it and it bolstered the league's popularity with fans and recruits, while providing a blueprint for the college game's eventual expansion into the television universe.

Like other southern conferences, the ACC was racially segregated in its early days. Maryland—the league's northern-most school—integrated its basketball team first, when Billy Jones broke the color barrier in December 1965.

The rest of the league dipped its toes in the waters and the league was fully integrated by 1971.

North Carolina State's David Thompson was one of those pioneering African American stars. Thompson led State to the 1974 NCAA title, the league's second. This team ended UCLA's seven-year title run in the Final Four.

An earlier tournament win, however, had an even more profound impact. NC State was ranked No. 1 when they advanced to the ACC Tournament title game against fourth-ranked Maryland. State edged Maryland 103-100 in overtime, in what is widely considered the greatest game in ACC history.

Another ACC Tournament title game that changed the college landscape took place at the end of the 1982 tournament, when top-seeded North Carolina and second-seeded Virginia squared off. North Carolina was led by James Worthy, Sam Perkins, and freshman superstar-in-waiting Michael Jordan, while Virginia had 7-4 Ralph Sampson, the nation's best player.

North Carolina led 44-43, with just under eight minutes left, when they went into a delay game. Dean Smith wanted Virginia's bigger but slower defenders to come out of their zone and wanted to draw Sampson away from the basket.

Virginia stayed back. North Carolina held the ball for over seven minutes, while an enraged national TV audience watched some of college basketball's best players stand around and do nothing.

The game ended with North Carolina winning 47-45. Both teams advanced to the NCAAs, with North Carolina winning it all.

The NCAA gave conferences permission to experiment with different rules the next season. The ACC went with a 30-second shot clock and a 17-foot, 9-inch 3-point shot.

The NCAA adopted a shot clock in 1985 and a 3-point shot in 1987.

Since its inception, the ACC has lost two original members—South Carolina in 1971 and Maryland in 2014. Georgia Tech joined the league in 1978, and Florida State joined in 1991. For the first forty seasons of its existence, the

ACC ranged in size from seven to nine teams and every basketball team played every other team twice in the regular season, a double round-robin.

Those days are long gone, as football-driven expansion has pushed the ACC to 15 teams, including traditional hoops powers Syracuse and Louisville.

2. Cameron Indoor Stadium. Opened in 1940 as Duke Indoor Stadium and named after Eddie Cameron in 1972, Cameron is college basketball's most iconic on-campus facility. *Sports Illustrated* ranked Cameron as the fourth best sports venue in the world in 1999.

Cameron Indoor Stadium is more than three-quarters of a century old. Its listed capacity of 9,333 is about half of that of the home courts of nearby rivals, the University of North Carolina and North Carolina State University. It lacks many of the amenities of newer facilities.

But it's still one of a kind.

Legend has it that basketball coach Eddie Cameron and football coach Wallace Wade sketched the outlines of the stadium on the back of a matchbook.

The Indoor Stadium opened on January 6, 1940. Princeton was the opponent.

It was a big deal. Local elected officials toured the facility and were impressed. The head of the Durham Chamber of Commerce used words like "colossal" and "wonderful."

The word "colossal" is not often used to describe Cameron. But it was a different world in 1940.

Cameron was designed by Philadelphia architect Horace Trumbauer, who had designed much of Duke's West Campus and James B. Duke's New York mansion.

Trumbauer had one concern about the proposed facility. He thought it was too ambitious. Surely, he told Duke, they would never need anything larger than 4,000 seats.

Duke didn't listen.

The facility was the largest basketball structure south of Philadelphia's Palestra. The opening-night crowd of 7,500 was the largest crowd to see a college basketball game in the South.

The Indoor Stadium cost $400,000 (or just under seven million in today's dollars) and was largely paid for by revenues from Duke's appearances in the 1939 and 1942 Rose Bowls and the 1945 Sugar Bowl.

A dedication ceremony was scheduled for 8 p.m., with the tipoff to follow. The keynote speaker was Robert B. House, a dean at the University of North Carolina, representing the Southern Conference.

House and assorted other dignitaries walked to the microphone at exactly eight, at which point the lights went out.

Something about a bad fuse. It took 10 minutes to get them back on.

Duke's Glenn Price had the first point ever scored in the building, a free throw. A few minutes later, he made the first field goal, putting Duke up 3-0.

Princeton tied the game 16-16 at the half but Duke pulled away late, using a 9-0 run to fuel a 36-27 win.

Price led everyone with 13 points.

Everett Case took over as head coach at North Carolina State for the 1946-47 season and sparked such enthusiasm for the sport that the 1947 Southern Conference Tournament was hastily moved from Raleigh's 4,000 seat-capacity Memorial Coliseum to the Duke Indoor Stadium.

Duke hosted two Southern Conference Tournaments, both won by NC State. Reynolds Coliseum, with a 12,400-seat capacity, opened on the NC State campus for the 1949 season and the Southern Conference—and then ACC—Tournament was moved there.

The name change for the stadium was precipitated by Eddie Cameron's announcement that he was retiring as athletic director in 1972. Cameron had been athletic director at Duke since 1951, following a coaching career at Duke that started in 1928.

The newly-christened Cameron Indoor Stadium had its critics. In 1973, television analyst Billy Packer said, "Duke has the worst gym in the ACC. An 18-year-old boy today is impressionable. And the Duke gym doesn't make a good impression on someone who is deciding where to play college basketball."

Duke began sprucing up Cameron but didn't embark on a full-scale renovation until 1989. Yet Duke has resisted calls to fully replace Cameron with something more modern and nothing resembling a new arena is on the horizon.

Combine the noise and intimacy of Cameron with hall-of-fame coaches and All-America players and you have lots of Duke wins. Through the 2015-16 season Duke has an 847-157 record in Cameron. That's a winning percentage just over 84 percent. Duke is 364-102 in ACC competition. The team has had one losing season at Cameron—a 7-8 mark in 1944—and 18 undefeated seasons there. The Blue Devils have scored 100 or more points 127 times in Cameron. Opponents have done so six times.

Coach Vic Bubas had an eight-year run of 76-5 at home in the 1960s. Bill Foster's last three Duke teams went 32-3 at Cameron. Mike Krzyzewski has had four home winning streaks in excess of 40 games, with 46 consecutive wins (1997–2000) being the best to date.

The first nationally-televised game from Cameron was Duke's 69-64 win over Marquette in 1979. The establishment of ESPN later that year upped the ante. Most of Duke's home games are now nationally televised.

Mike Krzyzewski led his team to 46 consecutive wins (1997–2000) at Cameron Indoor Stadium. (AP Photo/Grant Halverson)

3. The Blue Devils. But it doesn't mean what you think. Despite the horns, the pitchfork, and the tail of the iconic mascot, the nickname has no satanic implications.

To understand the full implications of the nickname, we have to go back to World War I, which the United States entered in 1917, allied with France, among others.

The United States needed to sell war bonds to finance the war effort.

One of the most popular solicitations involved speeches made by a group of elite French Alpine soldiers, the *Chausseurs Alpins* (Alpine Hunters), who toured the United States.

The Alpine Hunters wore distinctive blue uniforms, complete with capes and berets. They became known as the Blue Devils.

It's not clear if the Blue Devils appeared at Trinity College (Trinity College became Duke University in 1924). But they were so well known in the United States that Irving Berlin wrote a popular song about them called "The Blue Devils of France," which praised their courage and panache.

Trinity's athletic teams had not had an official nickname prior to World War I, going by such unofficial names as "The Fighting Methodists" or "The Blue and White."

Trinity was re-instituting football after a quarter-century gap, and the "Fighting Methodists" wasn't going to scare anybody. The school paper, the *Trinity Chronicle*, pushed for something more fearsome, and Blue Devils became a favorite option. Many returning students were war veterans, so they knew all about the courage and honor associated with the Blue Devils.

Trinity's athletic teams became the Blue Devils in 1922.

4. The Cameron Crazies. It's not clear when the name was first used, although it was in widespread use by the middle 1980s.

The Duke students are situated at courtside, only a few feet from the court—a pretty good place to make noise in a venue that barely holds 9,000.

Cameron was loud long before it officially became Cameron, in 1972. After a December 1964 game against Michigan, Duke star Jack Marin compared the volume to a jet aircraft taking off.

Gary Melchionni described it after a 1972 win over North Carolina.

"The noise level reached the white-noise stage, where it really isn't noise, it's something else."

Television made the Crazies nationally famous, as more and more games were broadcast and antiseptic, modern arenas moved students away from the action in favor of sedate season-ticket holders.

NBC's Al McGuire showed up for a game in 1979 with a whip and a pith hat, playfully riffing on the Crazies' reputation as animals.

The students took a PR hit in 1984, when Maryland came to town. Maryland player Herman Veal had been accused of sexual improprieties and the students littered the floor with underwear and condoms when Veal was introduced.

The students were pilloried in the press, especially by the *Washington Post*. Duke president Terry Sanford responded with an open letter to the students, imploring them to "think of something clever but clean, devastating but decent, mean but wholesome, witty and forceful but G-rated for television."

The so-called Uncle Terry Letter reset the switch and has served as the template for the Crazies for more than three decades.

Contrary to popular belief, much of what comes from the Crazies is not spontaneous. Cheer sheets are in evidence and television cameras do not go unnoticed.

The Cameron Crazies prepare to cheer Duke on to another victory.
(AP Photo/Gerry Broome)

And every Duke graduate swears the Crazies are nothing like they were back in the day.

But they are invariably loud, usually clever, and frequently intimidating to opponents.

In an example of one of the more unique circumstances, UNC's Steve Hale sat out a 1986 game with a collapsed lung. The Cameron Crazies pointed at Hale, chanting "in-hale, ex-hale, in-hale, ex-hale."

Even Hale thought it was funny.

The Cameron Crazies aren't the only student section known as a Sixth Man. But they're on every short list. Any time another university cheering section wants to extol its quality, it compares itself to the Cameron Crazies.

5. The winningest coach in men's D-I history, Mike Krzyzewski has been Duke's head coach since he replaced Bill Foster in 1980.

The median age in the United States is just under 38. If we assume that toddlers don't really follow college basketball, then that means more than half of US college basketball fans have no memory of Duke basketball before Krzyzewski arrived.

Through the end of the 2016 season Duke has played 2,951 games. Krzyzewski has coached 1,232 of them. He's coached over 55 percent of the games Duke has played in Cameron Indoor Stadium and almost 70 percent of Duke's regular-season ACC games. His teams have won all of Duke's NCAA titles, 13 of the school's 19 ACC Tournament titles, and have accounted for 12 of Duke's 16 Final Four appearances.

It almost didn't happen.

Krzyzewski was the ultimate stealth candidate. The three candidates to replace Foster were believed to be Mississippi coach Bob Weltlich, Old Dominion coach Paul Webb, and Duke assistant Bob Wenzel.

One local columnist was so certain this was the final list that he guaranteed that Foster's replacement would answer to "Coach W."

Duke athletic director Tom Butters and Indiana coach Bob Knight were friends. Weltlich had been an assistant under Knight at both Army and Indiana and it was natural that Butters would ask Knight about Weltlich.

Somewhere in the phone conversation Butters asked Knight if there was anyone else Duke should think about.

Krzyzewski had played for Knight at Army and coached for him one year at Indiana, before taking the head job at West Point.

Krzyzewski was coming off a 9-17 season at Army and was 73-59 overall, with one NIT appearance.

But Knight told Butters that Krzyzewski had the best young basketball mind in the country and that he has "all of my virtues and none of my flaws."

Butters brought Krzyzewski in for an interview. Krzyzewski thought he nailed it but left without an offer. Iowa State was interested in Krzyzewski but he had been holding them off.

Krzyzewski headed for the Raleigh-Durham airport and what he felt was a likely date with Ames, Iowa.

Back at Duke, Butters was telling assistant AD Steve Vacendak that Duke had found its man.

Vacendak's response? "Then why are we letting him get on a plane?"

Butters sent Vacendak to the airport to find Krzyzewski.

The deal was done. And that local scribe? He claimed he was right. Krzyzewski was Coach Who.

The school newspaper headlined "Krzyzewski: this is not a typo."

Krzyzewski was 33 years old.

Krzyzewski didn't exactly inherit a bare cupboard. His first Duke team had three future NBA players—forwards Gene Banks and Kenny Dennard and guard Vince Taylor.

Duke finished 17-13 in 1981 and made the NIT. But Banks and Dennard were seniors and Taylor was a junior and there wasn't much behind them.

Recruiting at Duke and the ACC is much different from recruiting at a military academy, and it took Krzyzewski some time to figure things out. He targeted too many players early on. His first two classes brought in a bunch of complementary players, which is nice if they have top-tier talent to complement.

Krzyzewski's second Duke team may have been the worst team in Duke history. They went 10-17 (4-10 in the ACC) and were outscored by an average of 6 points per game, the worst differential ever for Duke.

Duke lost at home to Appalachian State and lost at home 40-36 to a mediocre Maryland team, in what may have been the worst game ever played in Cameron Indoor Stadium.

And that was with Taylor leading the ACC with 20.3 points per game.

Krzyzewski desperately needed help, and he responded with a class that likely saved his career— forwards Mark Alarie and Jay Bilas, wing David Henderson, and most importantly guard Johnny Dawkins.

It's difficult to overstate the importance of Dawkins. A lightning-quick and highly skilled 6-foot-2 lefty, Dawkins was a McDonald's All-American. He turned down hometown Maryland and Big East powers like Villanova.

Johnny Dawkins finishes a reverse dunk for two of his 2,556 Duke points. (AP Photo)

"I grew up an ACC fan and always saw myself playing in the league," Dawkins told me years later. "I remembered Duke's great teams from the late 1970s, so I knew the school could compete. The academic reputation was terrific, but, ultimately, it was the people who sold me, especially Coach K. He did such a great job of recruiting me as an individual, painting a vision for my future. He was fiery, competitive, and knew where he wanted to go and how to take us there."

Bilas told a similar tale. "He explained how he would build the program, how we would win. I trusted him. It's as simple as that."

Krzyzewski started four freshmen in a veteran league that included seniors like Ralph Sampson at Virginia and Thurl Bailey at NC State.

It was a rough introduction. Alarie said Krzyzewski threw the freshmen into "the deep end of the pool."

Duke did have a promising win at improved Maryland. But there was a home loss to Wagner College, losses to North Carolina by 21 and 24 points, and an overall 3-11 ACC regular season.

Duke hit rock bottom in the ACC Tournament, opening against Sampson and second-ranked Virginia. If it had been a boxing fight, the referee would have stopped it early.

By the time the carnage was over, the scoreboard read 109-66.

It was the worst loss since the Taft Administration. The worst in school history had come back in 1913, when Trinity lost to Washington and Lee 90-15.

The loss to Virginia ended Duke's season at 11-17, tying the previous season's record for most losses.

Krzyzewski remains the only Duke coach to have consecutive losing seasons since Duke joined the Southern Conference in 1928.

Twenty-five miles down the road, NC State was celebrating a national title under Jim Valvano, who started at NC State within days of Krzyzewski's arrival at Duke.

The comparison was not flattering.

Butters was inundated with phone calls and letters, demanding that he fire Krzyzewski. Big donors threatened to pull away their checkbooks. It got ugly.

Few would have blamed Butters for firing a 36-year-old coach who was 38-47 at Duke.

But Tom Butters wasn't easily intimidated.

For the second time, he rolled the dice on Mike Krzyzewski. He not only kept him, but he even extended his contract.

Butters almost certainly knew of the immediate aftermath of that 43-point ACC Tournament debacle, when the Duke coaches and support staff retired to an Atlanta restaurant to lick their wounds.

It was there that a staffer proposed a toast. "Here's to forgetting tonight."

Krzyzewski interrupted. "Here's to never forgetting tonight."

Duke won its next 16 games against Virginia.

The callow freshmen of 1983 turned into veterans in 1984, augmented by the arrival of point guard Tommy Amaker, an elite defender and ball distributer.

The biggest wins came in the ACC Tournament. The fourth-seeded Blue Devils edged Georgia Tech in overtime to advance to a semifinal match against North Carolina.

The Tar Heels were coming off a 14-0 ACC regular season and were ranked number one in the nation. Their lineup was led by National Player of the Year Michael Jordan and fellow first-team All-American Sam Perkins.

But Duke had played Carolina tough twice, losing a week earlier in Chapel Hill in double overtime only after missing a crucial foul shot late in regulation that would have sewn up the win.

Duke pulled off the upset, 77-75, matching every haymaker with one of their own.

Mark Alarie scored 21 points for Duke. "This was a watershed," he said. "There was no more questioning ourselves. We knew we could beat anybody."

This would be Duke's last win of the season. The exhausted Blue Devils lost in the ACC Tournament title game to Maryland, got a bye in the first round of the NCAA Tournament, and lost in the round of 32 to Washington.

But a corner had been turned. There would be no more talk about replacing Krzyzewski, who turned Duke into a national contender, then a perennial national contender, and ultimately into an institution.

It hasn't all been smooth sailing since then though. Krzyzewski underwent back surgery in 1994. Always a fierce competitor (which is usually an asset), Krzyzewski disregarded medical advice and came back too early from surgery.

On Duke's trip back from the Rainbow Classic in late December, Krzyzewski suffered through an agonizing flight, coached two more games in pain, and went on a medical leave of absence that eventually extended through the season.

He was replaced for the duration by his top assistant, Pete Gaudet.

Duke was 9-3 when Krzyzewski shut it down but finished 13-18, the most losses in school history.

Eight of the team's losses under Gaudet were by five or fewer points, including double-overtime losses at home to Virginia and North Carolina.

Duke missed the NCAA Tournament for the only time since that 1983 season.

Two years later Duke captured the ACC regular-season title and four years later made it to the NCAA title game.

What makes Mike Krzyzewski so successful? Certainly, recruiting is a big part of his success. It's been said that 90 percent of the time the team that gets off the bus with the most talent will win.

Duke usually gets off the bus with the most talent. Duke has had at least one McDonald's and/or *Parade* All-America team member, beginning with that Dawkins-Alarie class. Krzyzewski has sent over 50 players to the NBA.

Why? Krzyzewski has a rare ability to articulate a vision and get people to buy into it.

The passion is obvious to even casual fans. Insiders remark on his organizational abilities, attention to detail, and time-management skills. He's disciplined but flexible, prepared but adaptable, and skilled in tactics and strategy, means and ends.

After a dismal effort at Virginia in 1991, Krzyzewski called a practice as soon as his team got off the bus back at Duke. "That's why Coach K is so good," Bobby Hurley told me. "It was his way of saying this was unacceptable."

Dennard, who played one season for Krzyzewski, spoke admirably of his coach.

"People are sometimes surprised to see this, but he was very patient. He was a teacher. If the efforts were there, he would work with you over and over. But the effort had to be there."

Tom Butters summed up Krzyzewski for me in 2008.

"Mike's a great basketball coach but he'll never be as good a basketball coach as he is a person. In fact, I don't think of him as a coach. He's an academician, a counselor, someone who cares about the kids who play for him as much as we care about our kids."

6. The University of North Carolina. There's a certain amount of subjectivity here. But not much. The (at least) two annual meetings between these programs draw national attention. Not sometimes. Not most of the time. All of the time.

The Tar Heels are not Duke's most common opponent, though the teams have played each other a total of 242 times through 2016. Duke has actually played NC State 245 times (with Duke winning 146 games) and Wake Forest 245 times (with Duke winning 167 games).

But ESPN doesn't fall all over itself when Duke plays Wake Forest.

There are a number of reasons why this is the case. The two schools are located a mere eight miles apart, in adjacent counties. Rival fans share jobs, churches, neighborhoods, and families. Wins and losses stick.

That explains why the two schools are local rivals.

But not why they are national rivals.

Through 2016, the NCAA has contested 77 NCAA Tournaments. North Carolina has competed in 47, Duke in 40. You have to go back to 1974 to find a season in which neither school was in the Big Dance.

They've also won once they've gotten there. North Carolina has participated in 19 Final Fours and Duke has been in 16. Beginning in 1963, North Carolina has been in 17 Final Fours and Duke has been in 16, with only an overlap in 1991. That means well more than half of the Final Fours since then have included at least one of these two teams. The ACC has won 13

NCAA titles. Duke has five of them, North Carolina has five of them, and everyone else has three.

North Carolina began taking basketball seriously a few years before Duke and ran up a 17-2 edge in head-to-head matchups, including 16 straight before Eddie Cameron took over the reins at Duke. Since then, it has been UNC 117, Duke 106, through 2016.

Both teams have had brief periods of dominance but never long enough to tip the scales very much, one way or the other. Duke's longest winning streak in the series was eight straight contests in the 1950s. Mike Krzyzewski–led teams won 11 of 12 from 1999 until 2003 and 15 of 17 going into the end of the 2006 season, when UNC started a 6-1 run against Duke.

UNC's longest period of dominance in the rivalry after that 1920s period was a 16-1 run in the 1970s, corresponding with some of Dean Smith's best teams.

The AP poll began in the 1948-49 season. The last time neither Duke nor North Carolina was ranked when they met was February 27, 1960. That's a streak of 142 games. However, North Carolina was ranked 12th in the UPI (coaches) poll; AP only went 10 deep in those days. The last game between the teams in which neither team was ranked in either national poll was 1955.

At least one of the schools has been ranked by AP in 161 of their first 175 matches. Both teams have been ranked 76 times.

These games matter on the local, regional, and national stage.

There have been some doozies, including 13 overtime contests, nine of which have been won by Duke. The rivalry has included epic comebacks, unexpected beat-downs, last-second heroics, and standout performances by some of the best players in college history.

Best game ever? It depends on which shade of blue one wears. There was the 1974 game in which North Carolina overcame an 8-point deficit in 17 seconds and won in overtime. Or Duke's 87-86 triple-overtime win in 1968. Or North Carolina's 97-73 win over top-ranked Duke in 1998. Or unranked Duke's 87-83 win over third-ranked North Carolina in Vic Bubas's final home game in 1969.

Or a dozen more candidates, two dozen, three dozen in what is college sports' greatest rivalry.

7. Christian Laettner scored 407 points in 23 NCAA Tournament games from 1989 through 1992. Duke won 21 of these games, with Laettner providing the winning points in the final seconds three times.

This doesn't necessarily mean Laettner was the greatest player in NCAA Tournament history. He played in an era when freshmen were eligible and teams could play as many as six tournament games in a season. He played with a shot clock and a 3-point shot.

UCLA's Lew Alcindor (later Kareem Abdul-Jabbar), by contrast, played only 12 games in three seasons. But UCLA won all of them, with Alcindor averaging 25.3 points and 16.8 rebounds per game. Oscar Robertson (Cincinnati) averaged 32.4 points in 10 NCAA Tournament games.

None of this is to diminish Laettner's accomplishments. You don't get to play 23 tournament games unless your team wins games, and Laettner helped Duke win lots of games. A strong case can be made that Laettner is the greatest tournament player in the modern age.

Laettner came to Duke from the Buffalo suburbs, a skinny, 6-foot-11 post player. By the time he left, Duke had won 123 games, making Laettner and classmate Brian Davis the first Duke class to average over 30 wins per season.

Laettner first made a lasting impact on the big stage in the 1989 East Region title game, which pitted second-seed Duke against top-seed Georgetown.

This was John Thompson's last great Georgetown team, which was 29-4 at the time and ranked second in the nation. Georgetown's best player was Charles Smith, but the scariest was center Alonzo Mourning, the nation's top freshman. In today's terms, Mourning was a "rim protector," an elite shot blocker who routinely disrupted opposing offenses.

Laettner played with an intensity that few could match. He went right at Mourning, outscoring him 24 to 11 and outrebounding him 9 to 5. Laettner hit 9 of 10 from the field and 6 of 7 from the foul line, as Duke won 85-77.

Laettner didn't have much of a chance to build on this in the Final Four, fouling out in 21 minutes, with 13 points and 7 rebounds, as Duke lost to Seton Hall.

Senior star Danny Ferry graduated after the 1989 season, and Duke subsequently retooled behind Laettner, freshman point guard Bobby Hurley, and a trio of senior starters—Phil Henderson, Robert Brickey, and Alaa Abdelnaby.

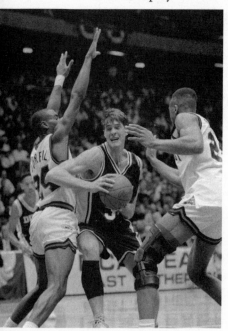

Christian Laettner splits a double team. (AP Photo/Bill Kostroun)

Abdelnaby had been a talented but erratic player his first three seasons at Duke. He finally put it together as a senior, which allowed Laettner to play away from the basket.

Duke beat Georgia Tech twice in the regular season and entered the final week of the regular season in first place. But the Blue Devils lost a high-profile game on the road against perhaps the best team in Clemson history, 97-93, despite Laettner's 25 points and 12 rebounds.

Duke followed with a desultory 12-point loss at home against North Carolina and a loss in the ACC Tournament semifinals to Georgia Tech, after which an angry Henderson could be heard calling his teammates "crybabies."

Three losses in four games hardly presaged a deep March run. But Duke came from behind to beat St. John's in a second-round game and got on one of those magical March runs. Laettner had 24 points and 14 rebounds as the third-seeded Blue Devils eased past UCLA into the East Region title game against the top-seeded Connecticut Huskies.

Abdelnaby had the best game of his career, finishing with 27 points and 14 rebounds.

Duke led by 11 early and nine in the second half. But Brickey went down and out with a hamstring pull and UConn fought back in a fiercely-contested game that saw 17 lead changes and 16 ties.

Chris Smith hit a 3 for the Huskies with :09 left for the tie. Abdelnaby missed at the buzzer and the game went into overtime.

Connecticut took a 78-77 lead on two Nadav Henefeld foul shots with 1:28 left. Each team had some empty possessions before Connecticut deflected a Hurley pass out of bounds. UConn just missed regaining possession by inches.

Duke called timeout with 2.6 seconds left. Krzyzewski called a play but ad-libbed when he saw that Laettner wasn't being guarded on the inbounds pass. Krzyzewski screamed "special," a play in which the inbound passer would find an open spot and get the ball back for the final shot.

"I got an anxiety feeling in my stomach," Laettner said after the game. "But once the play started, I was ready to go."

Laettner passed to Davis, got the ball back, and buried a 15-foot jumper.

The Blue Devils had completed the win, 79-78.

Laettner ended with 23 points, shooting 7 of 8 from the field.

Duke advanced to its third consecutive Final Four.

Duke hammered Arkansas 97-83 in one semifinal, overcoming a 69-62 deficit with a game-ending 35-14 run. Henderson's 28 points and Laettner's 19 points and game-high 14 rebounds led the way.

Duke met UNLV in the title game, in what might have been the worst two hours in Duke basketball history. Abdelnaby said later that his most vivid memory of that game was turning his neck and watching one Vegas player after another blowing by him on the way to a layup.

Laettner didn't play especially well, finishing with 15 points and 9 rebounds. But no one else played well either. That's how you end up on the wrong end of a 103-73 beat-down.

The loss was Duke's fourth in the title game, having played in eight Final Four matchups and 15 NCAA appearances, all without a title.

With three senior starters departing, 1991 didn't look like the year to change that narrative.

But everybody got better, including role players like Thomas Hill, Billy McCaffrey, Brian Davis, and Greg Koubek; Hurley; and especially Laettner, who went from second-team All-ACC in 1990 to second-team All-America in 1991. The addition of freshman Grant Hill injected elite athleticism.

Laettner was Duke's best player. His passion for winning inspired his teammates, but his tactics sometimes left something to be desired.

Hurley complained to Krzyzewski about Laettner's verbal bullying and Krzyzewski told Hurley he was talking to the wrong person.

Hurley and Laettner worked it out.

Duke swept North Carolina and captured the regular-season title. But the highlight may have been a mid-February home game against LSU and their imposing center Shaquille O'Neal.

Laettner dominated O'Neal, hitting from outside and driving by O'Neal when he tried to guard him on the perimeter. Laettner had 24 points and 11 rebounds, O'Neal 15 points and 10 rebounds.

Duke won 88-70.

Laettner had a career-high 37 points in a 111-94 win over UNC-Charlotte and 19 points in a 90-85 win at Oklahoma that ended the Sooners' 51-game home-winning streak.

A week after defeating North Carolina in Chapel Hill to clinch the regular-season title, Duke met UNC again in the championship game of the ACC Tournament. North Carolina routed an overconfident and sloppy Duke team 96-74.

Krzyzewski told the team after the game that they were going to win the national championship in three weeks.

Duke put the loss in the rearview mirror and coasted to the Midwest Region title, winning by margins of 29, 15, 14, and 17 points.

Their reward was a semifinal match with UNLV, the bullies of the previous season, a team so dominant that *Sports Illustrated* wrote before the Final Four, "the question becomes not whether the Rebels will win their second straight championship but how easily they will do it."

UNLV was 34-0 and riding a 45-game winning streak.

Laettner and his teammates refused to accept this narrative.

Krzyzewski said that the key to pulling off the upset was to get off to a good start. "We needed to win the first few rounds. They needed to see where we were at."

Duke won the first few rounds. Hurley was confident and assertive and Laettner was the best player on the floor. Laettner scored nine points early, as Duke jumped to a 15-6 lead.

Vegas caught up and the teams traded baskets going into the half with UNLV leading 43-41.

Vegas started double-teaming Laettner in the second half, but that opened up opportunities for his teammates. The favorites had so dominated their regular-season opponents that they had little experience with tight games, while the ACC-tested Blue Devils lived for close games.

It was as close as it could be, tied at 77 late, when Thomas Hill missed a bank shot. Grant Hill kept the rebound alive, and Laettner grabbed it and drew the foul.

The clock read 12.7 seconds left, plenty of time for UNLV to pull off the win if Laettner wobbled.

He didn't wobble. Both free throws swished through the net.

Vegas could only get off a desperation shot that missed badly.

Laettner ended with 28 points (9-14 from the field) and seven rebounds and helped hold UNLV star Larry Johnson to 13 points, barely half his season average.

Losing coach Jerry Tarkanian cited Laettner as the key.

"They didn't have anyone our center could guard and that changed our whole defense. Other teams have tried to do that but they didn't have anyone as good as Laettner."

The 79-77 win is widely regarded as the biggest win in Duke history.

But it didn't end the season.

Kansas had upset North Carolina in the other semifinal. It would have been easy for the exhausted Blue Devils to overlook the underdog Jayhawks. But most of the Duke team had been to the Final Four and come home empty, some several times.

There was no letdown against Kansas. Duke led most of the game, 72-65, winning it all for the first time.

Laettner led Duke with 18 points and 10 rebounds. He finished the six-game tournament with 125 points, shooting just over 61 percent from the field.

He was named Final Four Most Outstanding Player.

Duke returned six of its top eight players for 1992, including Laettner, Hurley, and both Hills.

The Blue Devils fought through a series of injuries to capture both the ACC regular-season and tournament titles.

Duke opened as the favorite to win it all and did nothing to dispel the notion with three double-digit wins, in which Laettner scored 22, 19, and 16 points.

Kentucky was Duke's East Region opponent. It was led by All-America post player Jamal Mashburn and a group of hungry role players determined to return Kentucky to its former glory.

The game is considered one of the greatest college basketball games ever played and will be covered in more detail elsewhere in the book.

But Laettner solidified his reputation that day, both in good and bad ways. In the second half, Laettner drew a foul on Kentucky forward Aminu Timberlake, who ended the play flat on his back.

Laettner stepped on Timberlake, a clear example of taunting, for which he was assessed a technical foul. Over the years this move has morphed into a vicious stomp and the genesis for a cottage industry of Laettner hatred, including an ESPN film entitled *I Hate Christian Laettner*.

Laettner stayed in the game and famously hit a buzzer-beater in overtime, giving Duke a pulsating 104-103 victory. Laettner ended the game making all 10 of his field goals (one 3-pointer) and all 10 of his free throws, for 31 points.

Laettner struggled early in the Final Four, especially in the first half against Indiana. Duke fell behind 39-27, and it was Hurley who led the comeback.

Laettner never found his shooting touch against the Hoosiers, finishing with only eight points. But he did pull down a game-high 10 rebounds as Duke won 81-78.

Michigan's freshman-laden team won the other semifinal. The legendary Fab Five helped steer Michigan to a one-point lead over Duke at the half and hung close until Duke pulled away in the middle of the second half, winning 71-51.

Christian Laettner ended his college career playing like Christian Laettner, with 19 points and seven rebounds. He was named to the All Final Four team.

Duke became the first team since UCLA in 1973 to repeat as national champions.

Bobby Hurley, who played three seasons with Laettner, praised his former teammate's approach, "He had a tremendous amount of confidence. He was not afraid of the moment."

8. J.J. Redick scored 2,769 points for Duke in a career that lasted from 2002-03 through 2005-06. The second-leading scorer in ACC history, Jonathan Clay Jr., aka Jonathan Jr., aka J.J. Redick, might be the best long-range shooter in ACC history.

Redick came to Duke from Cave Spring, Virginia, a suburb of Roanoke. Redick was a Duke fan during the Laettner-Hurley-Grant Hill era and decided he wanted to play basketball for Duke before he entered middle school.

Redick scored 43 in the Virginia high school state championship and was named Most Valuable Player of the 2002 McDonald's All-Star game, after leading all scorers with 26 points.

Still, there were skeptics. For one, they argued, Redick prepped in the Virginia mountains, and also, nobody plays defense in the McDonald's All-Star game. Maybe Redick was a one-trick pony.

Redick proved the critics wrong, scoring 20 points in his third college game, a neutral-court win over UCLA.

Redick went from promising talent to legend in the 2003 ACC Tournament. Duke trailed NC State by 15 points with 10 minutes left in the championship match before Redick scored 23 points in the final 10:05, leading Duke to an 84-77 victory, its fifth straight ACC Tournament title.

"That's the reason I came to Duke, to continue the tradition of being one of the top programs in the country," he said.

Redick scored 16 and 26 points in his first two NCAA Tournament games, wins over Colorado State and Central Michigan, but shot only two for 16 in a Sweet Sixteen loss to Kansas.

Redick's only Final Four appearance came in 2004. This was perhaps the most balanced team in Krzyzewski's Duke tenure, and during this particular game it showed. Five starters scored in double figures, led by Redick's 15.9 points per game and freshman Luol Deng's 15.1.

The team's glue was senior point guard Chris Duhon. He averaged 10 points per game but led Duke in minutes played, assists, and steals. He also provided senior leadership to a young team.

Duke finished first in the ACC but lost in the finals of the ACC Tournament, to Maryland in overtime.

Duke defeated Alabama State, Seton Hall, Illinois, and Xavier to capture the South Region. Deng was voted Most Outstanding Player, but Redick aided him with 65 points in the four games.

Duke lost to Connecticut 79-78 in the Final Four after leading much of the game, an eight-point lead with three minutes left squandered after all three Duke centers fouled out. Redick finished with 15 points.

Duhon graduated, Deng went to the NBA, and Krzyzewski told Redick that he needed to become more than just a shooter.

Redick lost weight, improved his conditioning, and refined his game, working on his passing and his ability to generate shots off his dribble.

He emerged as one of the nation's top players in 2005, leading the ACC with 21.8 points per game.

He did this with a wider repertoire. Redick was a career 91.2 percent foul shooter at Duke. Getting to the line meant points. Redick shot 111 foul shots in 33 games as a freshman. Two years later he went to the line 209 times in the same number of games. He shot 256 foul shots in 2006.

Redick again had a spectacular 2005 ACC Tournament, scoring 35 points (7 for 12 on 3-pointers) in a 76-69 win over NC State in the semifinals and 26 points in the title game, a 69-64 win over Georgia Tech.

Redick was named ACC Player of the Year, ACC Tournament MVP, and first-team All-America. He won the Rupp Award as national player of the year; Utah's Andrew Bogut won the other national POY awards.

Again, the season ended in a disappointment, a Sweet Sixteen loss to Michigan State, 78-68, in which Redick scored 13 points.

Until the final game, Redick's 2006 senior season had been a dream come true.

Duke began the season ranked No. 1 in the AP poll. Redick scored 30 to lead Duke to a 70-67 win over 11th-ranked Memphis to win the NIT Tip-Off tournament and 29 to lead Duke to a road win over 17th-ranked Indiana in the ACC–Big Ten Challenge.

On December 10 Duke played second-ranked Texas in a highly-touted match at New Jersey's Meadowlands.

Redick may have had the best regular-season performance in Duke history. Playing against a loaded Longhorns team that included future NBA star LaMarcus Aldridge, Redick hit nine of 16 from beyond the arc and 13 of 24 overall for 41 points total in a 97-66 blowout.

Duke broke the game open with a 16-0 run early in the second half, with Redick accounting for eight of those points.

"Before the game, one of the ball boys asked me how many points did I think I would score today and I told him, 'I honestly don't know,'" he said. "I never thought I'd get a career high. I came out in the warmups and the rims were nice and the nets were good. So I had a good feeling."

Duke started 17-0 before an 87-84 road loss to George-town. Redick matched his Texas total of 41 in the setback.

He had a 40-point game later that season in a win over Virginia. Redick and Dick Groat are the only Duke players to score 40 or more points three times in one season.

Redick spent much of the season chasing and catching Duke, ACC, and NCAA records. He passed Johnny Dawkins to become Duke's career scoring leader and then passed Dickie Hemric (Wake Forest) to become the ACC's career scoring leader. He set a since-broken (NC State, Scott Wood) ACC record by making 54 consecutive foul shots and broke Curtis Staples's (Virginia) NCAA record for career 3-pointers, all while enduring ferocious verbal abuse on the road.

Redick had another spectacular ACC Tournament, scoring 71 points in three games as Duke added the tournament title to its regular-season championship.

Redick still holds the ACC record for career points in the ACC Tournament, 225 points in 12 games, an average of 18.8 per game.

Redick repeated as ACC Player of the Year (receiving 105 of 108 votes) and ACC Tournament MVP, was unanimous first-team All-America, and won every national player of the year award.

J.J. Redick, the leading scorer in Duke history. (AP Photo/Gerry Broome)

Again, the ultimate goal of winning the NCAA Championship eluded Redick.

Duke was a curiously constructed team in 2006. Redick ended the season averaging 26.8 points per game, breaking Bob Verga's 39-year-old school record. Classmate Shelden Williams joined Redick as a first-team All-American, averaging 18.8 points and 10.7 rebounds per game.

But Duke never developed a consistent third scoring option. Two years after having five double-figure scorers, the 2006 Duke team joined the 1962 and 1982 teams as the only ACC-era Duke teams to have just two double-figure scorers.

This meant Duke was highly dependent on Redick. He scored 20 points to lead Duke over George Washington, into a Sweet Sixteen match with LSU.

The Tigers sent a platoon of strong, athletic defenders at Redick and hounded him into a three for 18 shooting game.

Redick scored his last points, a 3-pointer with 3:32 remaining, to give Duke its final lead, 52-51. LSU responded with an 11-2 run to sew up the 62-54 upset of the top-ranked Blue Devils.

North Carolina's Tyler Hansbrough passed Redick for the ACC career-scoring lead, while Travis Bader of Oakland University (in Michigan) passed him for career 3-pointers.

Redick still ranks fourth in NCAA career free-throw percentage.

The memories remain, of his range, as well as of the quickness and purity of a shot honed by countless hours in the gym. Then–Valparaiso coach Homer Drew called Redick's shot "a thing of beauty," while Michigan State's Tom Izzo marveled, "There's no ceiling to his range. I swear he can shoot a legitimate jump shot from near half-court."

9. Duke's Bobby Hurley had 1,076 assists in a four-year Duke career that ran from 1989 through 1993. Hurley played 140 games at Duke and averaged 7.7 assists per game. The Blue Devils played in the NCAA title game his first three seasons at Duke and won two NCAA titles with Hurley at point guard.

Bobby Hurley's father, Bob Hurley Sr., was a successful prep coach at St. Anthony High School in Jersey City. Bobby absorbed both Xs and Os from his father and a competitive drive from Jersey City gyms and playgrounds.

His prep teams went 115-5 and won four state titles.

He still wasn't the nation's top prep point guard. That distinction belonged to New York City's Kenny Anderson. Duke, North Carolina, and Georgia Tech all prioritized Anderson.

His father approached Dean Smith at UNC and Mike Krzyzewski with a question. Would you stop recruiting Anderson if my son wanted to commit to your program?

Smith declined, Krzyzewski accepted.

Anderson signed with Georgia Tech.

Establish a point-guard checklist, and Hurley hits the marks. He was quick, an excellent ball-handler, and had top-shelf court vision. He understood where the other nine players on the floor were and how they were best utilized. His passes could thread a needle.

He had some weaknesses. He too often went for the highlight-reel pass.

He also had bad body language, pouting when things went wrong.

As a freshman in 1990 he set a still-standing ACC record with 166 turnovers, five of them in a 30-point loss to UNLV in the title game. Hurley had a stomach bug during the game and

NCAA career assist record holder Bobby Hurley scrambles for a loose ball in Duke's win over St. John's in the second round of the 1990 NCAA Tournament. (AP Photo/Dave Martin)

nightmares about sharks for months afterwards (UNLV coach Jerry Tarkanian was known as "Tark the Shark").

Krzyzewski showed him a montage of bad-body-language footage and he got that straightened out. He also fixed his relationship with Christian Laettner by standing up to him.

Hurley would always be a high-risk, high-reward point guard. But the ratio improved, as did his shooting.

Two games stand out.

Duke advanced to the 1991 Final Four and Hurley got a chance to exorcise his UNLV demons. Playing with a toughness and poise absent a year earlier, Hurley consistently beat UNLV pressure to set up easy buckets, assisting on seven baskets, while turning it over three times. He hit arguably the biggest field goal of the game, a 3-pointer that cut UNLV's 76-71 lead to two points, with two minutes left.

"It was a critical possession," he said later. "It was the purest stroke I had felt."

Duke won 79-77.

"I thought Hurley was primed for the game," Krzyzewski told me later. "Bobby took it (1990) personally and I'm glad he did."

Hurley's crucial contribution in 1992 occurred in the Final Four, against Indiana. Duke fell behind 39-27 but Hurley led the comeback, hitting four first-half 3-pointers and scoring 16 points as Duke closed the gap, to 42-37 at intermission.

Hurley ended with 26 points and four assists in Duke's 81-78 win.

Hurley had nine points and seven assists as Duke defeated Michigan for the title. He was named Most Outstanding Player.

He had his best individual season as a senior, in 1993. Hurley averaged career highs in points (17.0) and assists (8.2), the latter still a school record. Late in the season he passed former NC State star Chris Corchiani to become the NCAA career leader in assists. He made every All-America first team for which he was eligible.

But team success eluded him. Duke had a hard time replacing Laettner, who had graduated, and Grant Hill was bothered much of the season with a bad toe.

Duke never really had a chance to win its third straight title. The Blue Devils opened with a 105-70 win over Southern Illinois, with Hurley hitting six of seven 3-pointers on the way to a 25-point game. But a bigger test was next, against California. Starting center Cherokee Parks went out in the first half with a sprained ankle and Duke fell behind 70-53.

Hurley led a comeback and Duke took a one-point lead late but ultimately fell 82-77.

Hurley ended his college tenure with a career-high 32 points.

10. The Dixie Classic was a holiday tournament held between 1949 and 1960 at Reynolds Coliseum on the campus of North Carolina State. It featured North Carolina's big four, plus four invited visitors.

NC State coach Everett Case and Raleigh sportswriter Dick Herbert came up with the idea for the three-day tournament held the week between Christmas and New Year's, North Carolina against the world.

Four outside teams—all high-profile programs—joined them. Oscar Robertson and Cincinnati came down in 1958, ranked No. 1, and left with two losses. Notables like Louisville, Utah, Michigan State, Minnesota, Brigham Young, Iowa, and DePaul competed over the years.

The format was simple. Four games were played each day, and everyone played three times. The North Carolina schools never played each other on the opening day, but after that the pairings were determined by who won and who lost.

The Dixie Classic was popular and successful. In a time when few college basketball games were telecast and inter-sectional competition was rare, the Dixie Classic was a source of bragging rights for the season.

The local schools did most of the bragging. NC State won seven of the dozen Dixie Classics, North Carolina captured three, and Duke and Wake Forest one each.

The closest a visitor came to taking home the title was in 1954, when NC State edged Minnesota 85-84 in the title game.

Duke's only Dixie Classic championship came in 1953, the ACC's inaugural season.

Duke opened with Oregon State. By 1953 standards, Oregon State might as well have been from Mars. Local newspapers treated them as exotic visitors, focusing on their trio of seven footers, the "Tall Firs."

Oregon State's 7-3 Swede Halbrook scored 23 points against Duke. But the smaller but quicker Blue Devils ran rings around the Tall Firs, beating them 71-61. Guards Joe Belmont and Rudy D'Emilio led Duke with 19 points each.

D'Emilio, a 5-11 senior from Philadelphia, keyed two more wins, scoring 23 points in an 83-66 win over Wake Forest and 23 in a 98-83 win over Navy.

The 98 points was the most points ever scored in a Dixie Classic championship game.

The title was an outlier for Duke, which only made the title game one other time, a 1960 loss to North Carolina. Duke's overall record in the Dixie Classic was 19-17.

The Dixie Classic ended after 1960 when it was revealed that NC State players had accepted money from gamblers to shave points in a number of games, some in the Dixie Classic; a UNC player was implicated as a go-between.

There was talk of reviving the Dixie Classic, but it never came to anything. The four North Carolina schools came up with the Big Four, which was held in Greensboro from 1970-71 through 1980-81.

Fans loved it, coaches' feelings ranged from ambivalent to worse, and the Big Four moved all over the calendar, playing as early as November 26, as late as January 5.

Duke went 9-13 but did win it all twice, during Bill Foster's last two seasons at Duke. The final Big Four was held in Mike Krzyzewski's first season at Duke.

11. Shane Battier won that award in 1999, 2000, and 2001. Only UNLV's Stacey Augmon (1989–1991) and Wake Forest's Tim Duncan (1995–1997) have duplicated that accomplishment.

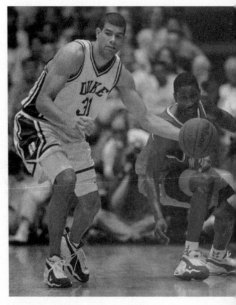

The 6-foot-8 Battier was the most versatile defender in Duke history. He ranks third in Duke career blocks (254), second in steals (266), and first in charges taken (111). He had eight blocks in an NCAA Tournament win over Kansas in 2000 and seven steals against Davidson as a freshman.

Battier's come-from-behind block on UNC's Joseph Forte's breakaway layup in the 2001 season might be the single most impressive defensive play in Duke history.

National Player of the Year Shane Battier in action. (AP Photo/Grant Halverson)

He did all this without being a defensive specialist. Battier averaged over 17 points per game in 2000 and almost 20 in 2001, when he led the title team with 7.3 rebounds per game.

It's no wonder Mike Krzyzewski called Battier "the most complete player I've ever coached."

12. Grant Hill's father Calvin played in four Pro Bowl games and two Super Bowls as a running back with the Dallas Cowboys. Grant's mother, Janet, was a suitemate of Hillary Rodham Clinton's at Wellesley College. Calvin Hill attended Yale and was the first Ivy League player selected in the first round of the NFL Draft.

Calvin Hill was the 1969 NFL Rookie of the Year and his son was the 1995 NBA Rookie of the Year.

Grant Hill played soccer growing up in the D.C. suburbs—his father ended his playing career with Washington—but committed to basketball at South Lakes High School in Reston, Virginia.

By the time he graduated in 1990 he was a McDonald's All-American and the prize of Duke's recruiting class.

Hill was a freshman on a team that included sophomore Bobby Hurley and junior Christian Laettner, three of the best players in Duke history.

He was an exceptional athlete, with a high basketball IQ.

His freshman season wasn't without some bumps in the road. Hill missed some time with a hip pointer and broke his nose in practice, but he was healthy when Duke entered the NCAA Tournament and advanced to the Final Four.

Duke was matched against top-ranked and undefeated UNLV, the same team that had mauled a much more experienced Duke team in the 1990 title game.

Hurley and Laettner returned from that team and both were much improved from the previous season, as were Thomas Hill, Brian Davis, and Billy McCaffrey.

But Grant Hill was something UNLV hadn't seen before, not from Duke.

Hill scored off the opening tap, a strong, athletic move to the basket that set an early tone.

He didn't have a great stat line that game, 11 points and five rebounds, right at his season average. But he absolutely shut down UNLV All-American Stacey Augmon, holding him to six points, 11 below his season average.

"This was the game when I realized I could be a pretty good defender," Hill recalled. "My versatility bothered him."

Duke defeated Kansas two nights later. Hill had the game's signature play, elevating into the stratosphere to not only control an errant Hurley pass in transition but to slam it home.

Hill ended that game with 10 points, eight rebounds, three assists, and two steals, typical for one of the most versatile players in Duke history.

That versatility was displayed in 1992, when Hurley went out with a broken foot in mid-season and Hill moved to point guard.

Duke's first post-Hurley game was at LSU, with Shaquille O'Neal. Hill had six assists to go along with 16 points and Duke won 77-67, the first of four wins in five games in Hurley's absence.

The injury bug bit Hill again, this time a high-ankle sprain, causing him to miss three games.

Hill's roommate Tony Lang played so well in his absence that, upon his return, Hill went to Krzyzewski and suggested that he would be fine coming off the bench in order for Lang to continue starting.

Hill played all three games as Duke captured the ACC Tournament. He scored 20 in the championship win over North Carolina.

He scored 72 points and grabbed 39 rebounds in Duke's six NCAA Tournament wins but is best remembered for throwing the pass that Christian Laettner converted into a basket to defeat Kentucky in overtime.

Hill started his junior season playing at an All-America level. But he sprained a big toe, missed six games, then played hurt and never really got healthy until he underwent postseason surgery.

Duke lost to California in the second round of the NCAAs, ending a streak of five consecutive Final Fours.

Despite the injury, Hill still averaged 18 points and was a consensus second-team All-America player.

Grant Hill's 1994 senior season was one of the best in Duke history.

Though the Blue Devils certainly weren't without talent—Hill's teammates included Lang, Cherokee Parks, Jeff Capel, and Chris Collins—it was not a national championship roster, and Hill carried that team on his back to within seconds of a national title.

Hill led Duke in points, minutes, assists (as a forward), and steals and was second in rebounds and blocks.

Hill had only made five 3-pointers in his first three seasons at Duke. But after Duke lost Hurley and Thomas Hill after the 1993 season, Grant worked on his perimeter game and made 39 3-pointers as a senior.

Collins said later of Hill's 1994 season, "He always made the right play and gave us confidence because we knew we had him on our side. He made us feel like we could do anything."

Hill did all this while excelling as a defender. Duke advanced to the Elite Eight as a two seed, where they met top-seeded Purdue in the Mideast Region title game.

The Boilermakers were led by 6-foot-8, 240-pound Glenn "Big Dog" Robinson, the nation's leading scorer and consensus National Player of the Year; Hill joined him as a first-team All-America player.

Robinson had just destroyed Kansas with 44 points.

Grant Hill scores over California's Jason Kidd in the 1993 NCAA Tournament. (AP Photo/John Swart)

Hill acknowledges that he had help from Duke's switching defenders, especially when he sat out five minutes of the second half with four fouls.

But he had Robinson most of the game and Robinson scored 13 points, shooting 6 for 22 from the field, missing all six of his 3-pointers.

Hill led everyone with 25 points as Duke defeated Florida 70-65 in the Final Four to advance to the championship, the fourth time in five seasons Duke was in the final game.

Their opponent was Arkansas, second-ranked in the national polls.

Duke led by as much as 10 points in the second half before suffering a Razorbacks comeback and falling 76-72.

Hill only scored a dozen points but led everyone with 14 rebounds.

13. Cameron Indoor Stadium was named for Eddie Cameron, the second-winningest coach in Duke history. Cameron won 226 games in his 14 seasons as head coach. But that's just the tip of the iceberg. Cameron also served as an assistant football coach at Duke as well as the head football coach and retired as the school's athletic director.

Trinity College became Duke University in 1924. School president William Preston Few felt that an increased athletic profile would help spread the news. By the end of the 1920s Duke had hired Wallace Wade to coach its football team, Jack Coombs to coach the baseball team, and Eddie Cameron to coach the basketball team. All three have on-campus facilities named after them.

Eddie Cameron was 24 years old when he started at Duke, as coach of the freshman football team, the freshman basketball team, and P.E. instructor. He had been captain of the football and basketball teams at Washington and Lee University.

Cameron was from Irwin, Pennsylvania, where his father was a coal-company executive. His father died in 1923. Cameron attended the funeral, took a train to Washington and Lee's football game against Virginia, and arrived at halftime of a scoreless game. Cameron told his teammates he wanted their fight, not their sympathy, and proceeded to score the only touchdown in a 7-0 win.

Cameron came to Duke at the behest of head football coach Jimmy DeHart, his former coach at Washington and Lee. He hoped to attend law school at Duke and coach but quickly realized that he couldn't juggle that many balls and gave up on the idea of becoming a lawyer.

Duke looked to Cameron, who made a positive impression quickly, to not only revive the basketball program but make it competitive in a league that included North Carolina and Kentucky.

Cameron's first Duke team went 12-8, then 18-2 in his second season. That team went 9-1 in the Southern Conference but lost to Alabama in the tournament title game.

Cameron did all this while continuing as an assistant coach for Wade's football program.

There weren't any postseason opportunities for much of Cameron's coaching career; the NIT started in 1938, the NCAA Tournament the following year.

The Southern Conference Tournament thus was the end point of the season and Cameron's teams captured 1938, 1941, and 1942, while losing in the championship game in 1929, 1930, 1933, 1934, and 1940, starting a tradition of Duke tournament success carried on by his successors.

Cameron's last Duke team was his best. Led by senior forward Ray Spuhler, Duke lost its third game and then went on a 14-game winning streak, which ended with a loss to George Washington.

Duke finished the regular season with three more wins and captured the Southern Conference Tournament with wins by 18, 9, and 11 points, putting Duke at 22-2.

There were no automatic qualifiers to the NCAA Tournament in those days. The eight teams were selected by region. Duke was bypassed for the southern slot in favor of a five-loss Kentucky team. Duke had flirted with the NIT but waited too long and missed out there.

The .916 winning percentage remained the school record until the 1986 team went 37-3.

And still, Eddie Cameron ended his basketball coaching career without ever coaching a single postseason game.

By the time the 1942 season ended the United States was involved in World War II. Wade had served in World War I and volunteered for service a second time.

Cameron, taking Wade's place in the interim, gave up his basketball duties to Gerry Gerard. Gerard had played football at Illinois but Cameron had seniority, and football was much higher on the pecking order than basketball.

Duke spent most of World War II training Navy officers and most of Cameron's football players were on the fast track out. Still, Cameron coached Duke to a 25-11-1 mark over four seasons and Duke's first bowl victory, 29-26, over Alabama in the 1945 Sugar Bowl.

Wade came back for the 1946 season and resumed his football duties. Gerard remained basketball coach, while Cameron became the athletic director.

Cameron held that position until his retirement in 1972, the year Duke Indoor Stadium was renamed Cameron Indoor Stadium. He was one of the prime movers in the establishment of the Atlantic Coast Conference in 1953, served on countless NCAA committees, and hired Vic Bubas as basketball coach in 1959.

14. The 2001 Duke Blue Devils. Senior forward Shane Battier won all of the national player of the year awards except the NABC award, which was won by Duke sophomore Jason Williams. Battier and Williams led Duke to a 35-4 mark and the school's third NCAA championship.

Returning everyone but Chris Carrawell from 2000's ACC championship team, Duke began the season ranked second nationally behind Arizona and never dropped lower than fourth. Duke's first three losses were by one, two, and two points, respectively, all to teams ranked in the top 12.

Battier was a 6-foot-8 senior and the nation's best defender.

He also was a 20-points-per-game-scorer, Duke's best rebounder, and an exceptional leader.

Williams was a 6-foot-2 guard who could get to the rim at will but also ran the team at a high level, creating shots for his teammates.

He would lead the ACC with 21.6 points per game, while adding 6.1 assists.

They had help. Center Carlos Boozer and forward Mike Dunleavy Jr. would go on to play almost 30 combined seasons in the NBA.

Fifth-year senior Nate James—a tough defender and long-range bomber—started most of the season at shooting guard but was replaced late in the season by 2001 ACC Rookie of the Year Chris Duhon.

Boozer was the only member of the six-player core rotation who was not a threat from downtown. The 2001 team would end the season by making 407 3-pointers, a still-standing school record.

This team had two of the greatest regular-season wins in school history. The first came on January 27, when second-ranked Duke visited eighth-ranked Maryland, the first of four memorable games between the two teams that season.

Duke trailed by 12 with a minute left.

But Williams scored eight straight points, James sent the game to overtime from the line, and Duke won 98-96.

Maryland won the rematch a month later in Cameron, 91-80. But the big news was a broken right foot suffered by Boozer, an indefinite absence only weeks before the beginning of the NCAA Tournament.

Krzyzewski shook things up. He replaced Boozer with quick center Casey Sanders, moved Duhon into the starting lineup, and brought James off the bench.

Sanders still didn't play as much as James, but he provided an injection of energy at the beginning of games. Duke went to Chapel Hill five days after losing Boozer and ran rings around the Tar Heels, winning 95-81.

Duke followed with easy wins in the ACC Tournament, 76-61 over NC State in the opener and 79-53 over North Carolina in the title game. But they only made it to the finals after a riveting semifinal win over Maryland 84-82 on a late James tip-in.

Duke entered the NCAAs ranked number one in the AP poll.

The Blue Devils opened with comfortable wins over Monmouth and Missouri.

While all this was going on, Boozer's broken foot was healing. He started practicing the week before the Sweet Sixteen and got back on the court against UCLA, 23 days after his injury.

Boozer scored two points in 22 minutes off the bench. Duke didn't need more, with Williams (34) and Battier (24) leading a 76-63 win.

Southern Cal had upset Kentucky to advance to the East title game. It was almost a carbon copy of the UCLA game, with Duke winning 79-69 behind Williams's 28 points and Battier's 20.

Boozer again played 22 minutes, scoring a single point.

Duke, Michigan State, Arizona, and Maryland comprised the 2001 Final Four, held in Minneapolis. The Blue Devils were matched against Maryland in the teams' fourth meeting of the season. A week of practice had helped Boozer, who made his first start since his injury. But it looked like his presence was for nothing after Maryland exploded to a 39-17 lead, pummeling Duke on the glass and pressing Duke into costly turnovers.

Duke rallied late in the half and cut it to 49-38.

Krzyzewski made some halftime adjustments. Juan Dixon had killed Duke in the first half, with 16 points. Krzyzewski put James on Dixon.

"We were looking to run plays to bail us out," Battier said following the game. "The best thing was for us just to play basketball and play our motion offense."

James shut down Dixon, holding him to three second-half points. Duke took the lead when Williams hit a 3-pointer to make it 73-72, with 6:49 left.

Then Boozer made his presence felt, with nine points in the final four minutes as Duke pulled away for a 95-84 win.

Battier led everyone with 25 points, two more than Williams. Boozer added an encouraging 19.

Krzyzewski saved his greatest praise for James.

"Our big guys played, offensively and defensively, their best game of the year," he said after the game. "But the biggest spark all night was Nate. He made big plays and he fought Juan Dixon hard all night."

Arizona defeated defending champion Michigan State 80-61 in the other semifinal.

Like Duke, fifth-ranked Arizona featured top-shelf NBA talent, including Gilbert Arenas and Richard Jefferson. They were on a mission to win for veteran head coach Lute Olson, who had lost his wife to cancer months earlier.

Neither team got much separation in the first half, which ended with Duke up 35-33.

In the second half, Dunleavy hit three 3-pointers in a 46-second span to put Duke up 50-39.

Arizona clawed back, an Arenas layup making it 68-65, with 5:28 left.

That was as close as they got.

Battier made the key plays down the stretch, including a follow shot making it 73-68, a tip-in that made it 75-70, a dunk that made the score 77-72, and a screen that freed Williams for a 3-pointer to make it 80-72.

The final was 82-72, giving Duke double-digit victory margins in all six of its NCAA Tournament wins that season, a deceptive statistic in some respects but also an indication of a certain killer instinct.

Dunleavy led Duke with 21 points, 18 of which came after intermission. But Battier's overall excellence—18 points, 11 rebounds, six assists, and two blocks—earned him the Most Outstanding Player award.

Boozer gave Duke 12 points and a dozen rebounds.

Williams added 16 points.

"It's complete," Battier said after the game. "All that's left for me is to ride off into the sunset on a white horse. I love my guys—we fought, we fought, it was a great year, and this is just the perfect way for us to end it."

15. Shelden Williams picked up that name in high school, when he blocked 16 shots in a single game, prompting a local writer to claim that Williams owned the lane and everyone else was a tenant. By the time he finished at Duke, Williams was one of the best shot blockers in ACC history.

Williams could dominate a game just as a rim protector. The national Defensive Player of the Year in 2005 and 2006, Williams blocked 422 shots at Duke, third only to Wake Forest's Tim Duncan and Georgia Tech's Alvin Jones in ACC annals. He is the only Duke player to ever have 100 blocks in a season and he did it three times. The 6-foot-9 Williams had eight or more blocks in a game five times, including a school-record 10 against Maryland in 2006; Cherokee Parks also had a 10-block game in 1994.

But Williams wasn't a specialist. He also grabbed 1,262 rebounds, first in school history. Williams led the ACC in rebounding in 2005 and 2006 and is the only Krzyzewski player to do so. Williams and Mike Gminski are the only players to lead Duke in rebounding four seasons.

He improved his offense every year, averaging 18.8 points per game as a senior in 2006, when he was consensus first-team All-America.

16. The 1991-92 team began the season at the top of the polls and held that spot all the way through a 34-2 season, which ended with Duke's second consecutive NCAA championship.

Duke returned the bulk of its 1991 national title team, including center Christian Laettner, forward Grant Hill, and point guard Bobby Hurley, three of the best players in ACC history.

All three have had their jerseys retired by Duke. The 1991 and 1992 teams are the only ones to include three Duke players with retired jerseys.

In 1992, Hurley was a junior point guard, a consummate playmaker. The 6-foot-8 Grant Hill, a sophomore, was arguably the most versatile player in Duke history, capable of playing every position except center, an attacking scorer and lock-down defender.

Then there was Laettner, Duke's alpha dog and the best player in college basketball. Laettner was 6-foot-11 and played like it, leading Duke in scoring (21.5) and rebounding (7.9), while blocking a shot a game. But he also shot almost 56 percent on 3-pointers (54-97) and led Duke in steals.

Laettner's defining characteristics were a fierce competitiveness and a supreme confidence that verged on arrogance.

The big three had plenty of help. Thomas Hill, a 6-foot-4 junior guard, was the team's unsung hero, a standout defender and wing rebounder and clutch shooter. In fact, he was Duke's second-leading scorer.

Add senior forward Brian Davis, sophomore forward Tony Lang, and freshman center Cherokee Parks and Duke was loaded.

Duke began the season ranked atop the AP poll.

The 1992 Duke team was more than just a talented college basketball team. With Laettner as the focal point, they were more like a traveling rock band—loved by many, hated by many, and ignored by few. The 1991 title team might have been the last Duke team that was a loveable underdog. The 1992 team was the season when Duke became college basketball's bullies.

Duke's run wasn't without some bumps in the road. Duke went to Chapel Hill on February 5 with a gaudy 17-0 mark, only two games really competitive, one an overtime win at Michigan against their Fab Five freshmen.

Hurley broke a bone in his right foot late in the first half, Laettner missed a contested layup at the buzzer, and the Tar Heels prevailed 75-73.

Second-ranked Oklahoma State also lost, and Duke held onto the top spot.

Hurley would miss five games and Duke didn't have a backup; combo guard Billy McCaffrey had transferred after the 1991 season, too late for Krzyzewski to recruit another point.

A trip to Baton Rouge loomed, against Shaquille O'Neal and nationally-ranked LSU. Krzyzewski inserted Lang into the lineup and moved Grant Hill to point guard.

How many teams move their power forward to point guard?

Hill handled the switch like a seasoned veteran, tallying 16 points and six assists. Laettner and O'Neal played to a draw and Duke pulled away late for a 77-67 victory.

Duke went 4-1 in Hurley's absence, the loss coming at Wake Forest, after Duke led by 10 in the second half. Duke had a chance to tie it late. Hill tried to hit Laettner on a floor-length in-bounds pass, but it curved to the left, out of Laettner's reach.

The loss dropped Duke to 21-2, still good enough to hold on to the top spot.

Hurley got back around the time Grant Hill injured an ankle, missing three games. Duke finished the regular season with an 89-77 win over North Carolina, Laettner scoring 26 in his home finale.

Everybody was healthy for the ACC Tournament, where Laettner and company took care of unfinished business, winning their first ACC Tournament title, with an emphatic 94-74 win over the Tar Heels.

Laettner scored 73 points in the three games.

Duke opened the NCAAs with double-digit wins over Campbell, Iowa, and Seton Hall.

Duke met Kentucky in the East Region finals. Under Rick Pitino, Kentucky was rebuilding after the scandal-plagued tenure of Eddie Sutton.

Pitino had 6-foot-8, 240-pound Jamal Mashburn and surrounded him with a group of tough, scrappy players who went on the court with a chip on their shoulders.

Kentucky came into the game 29-6, seeded second in the region and ranked sixth nationally.

Still, by this point, people were calling Duke's season the Victory Tour and few thought Kentucky could hang with Duke.

Their epic match remains one of the most famous in college basketball history and one with multiple narratives.

The Victory Tour rolled down the highway early, Duke leading 50-45 at intermission and extending the lead to 67-55 nine minutes into the second half.

But the Wildcats were perfectly designed to come from behind. They could press, they could hit 3-pointers, and they weren't inclined to go away easily.

Kentucky caught up. Duke started seniors Laettner and Davis and juniors Hurley and Thomas Hill, all four of whom had played in a lot of big games. They didn't get flustered easily.

But they were flustered.

Except Laettner. He survived a technical foul from stepping on Kentucky's Aminu Timberlake and kept Duke afloat.

Regulation ended at 93-93, after Hurley missed a late 3 that could have won it all.

The blue bloods traded baskets in overtime. Duke was first to 100 when Laettner hit a jumper to break a 98-98 tie.

Mashburn got an old-fashioned three-point play and it was 101-100 Kentucky, with 19.6 seconds left.

Laettner drew a foul with 7.8 seconds left and calmly drained both foul shots.

Duke got a stop against UNLV in a similar situation the previous season. But Kentucky's Sean Woods got into the lane and banked a prayer off the glass with 2.1 seconds left.

Timeout.

Krzyzewski was equal parts X and O and leader. "We're going to win this game and here's how we're going to do it," he said, while reminding Laettner that he would have time to take a dribble before launching the shot on which Duke's title hopes rested.

Laettner responded, "if [Grant Hill] makes the pass, I'll make the shot."

Duke ran the same play it had tried at the end of the Wake Forest game.

Hill threw a strike the second time around, a 75-foot strike. It helped that Pitino elected to not guard Hill, using the extra defender to double Laettner. But Laettner was 6-foot-11, his defenders 6-foot-6.

Laettner made the catch, faked, dribbled, and made the jumper, nothing but net.

"Grant threw a perfect pass, and I just concentrated on catching the ball," Laettner said following the game. "After I caught the ball, I tried to create some distance and shoot the ball up. I couldn't see the ball go through the hoop because all these kids were flying around."

Krzyzewski said that Duke had been part of a classic and that's still the case. Kentucky shot 57 percent from the field, hit 12 of 22 from beyond the arc, and turned it over only 12 times, while forcing Hurley into eight turnovers.

And still lost.

Laettner famously scored 31 points without missing a shot—Duke shot over 65 percent from the field. But Hurley's 22 points and 10 assists against Kentucky's relentless pressure were just as important.

The game may have been a classic, but it didn't win anything for Duke other than a chance to keep playing, at the Final Four in Minneapolis.

It did send Duke to its fifth consecutive Final Four, an accomplishment matched only by Cincinnati (1959–63) and bettered only by UCLA (1967–75).

Indiana was up first. The Hoosiers were coached by Krzyzewski's mentor, Bobby Knight. They had met once before in the NCAA, a 1987 Sweet Sixteen game won by IU on their way to Knight's third NCAA championship.

But the context had changed in five years. Krzyzewski had won two NCAA titles since Knight's last title and was no longer viewed as Knight's apprentice.

Laettner was exhausted against Indiana, perhaps more emotionally than physically. He was the senior constant on a team that had been handicapped by injuries throughout the season, he was a flashpoint for Duke fans and Duke enemies, and he was inundated with attention following the Kentucky game. In addition, he couldn't buy a basket; everything came up short.

Indiana led 39-27. But Hurley kept hitting 3s and Duke trailed only 42-37 at the break.

A 21-3 run early in the second half gave Duke some breathing room. But the injury bug bit again, as Brian Davis went out with a sprained knee.

Indiana clawed back and the final minutes featured huge plays by two end-of-the-bench reserves. Hoosiers guard Todd Leary hit a trio of 3-pointers in the final minute.

Grant Hill had fouled out by then and with Davis out, Krzyzewski went with sophomore Marty Clark, who was averaging less than three points per game. Clark hit five of six from the line in two minutes and Duke held on, 81-78.

Laettner scored eight points, his only single-digit game of the season. He did grab 10 rebounds.

Hurley led everyone with 26 points, including six of nine from beyond the arc.

Michigan edged Cincinnati in the other semifinal.

The Fab Five had pushed Duke into overtime earlier in the season and had had four months to improve. Michigan led 31-30 at the half, but Duke found another gear in the second half, one that Michigan did not have. The final was 71-51. Duke had become the first repeat champion since UCLA in 1973.

Laettner rallied for a 19-point, 7-rebound end to his college career. But Hurley's nine points and seven assists solidified his Final Four Most Outstanding Player status.

17. The 1978 Duke team advanced to the NCAA title game after finishing in last place in the ACC for three consecutive seasons. Duke went from 14 wins in 1977 to 27 in 1978, tying the school record for wins.

Duke's improbable 1978 run makes sense in retrospect. Junior guard Jim Spanarkel, sophomore center Mike Gminski, and freshman forward Gene Banks were all ACC rookies of the year, all three became All-America players, and they were the first three Duke players to score 2,000 career points. The trio combined for 6,414 points, 2,781 rebounds, and 887 assists at Duke and played 25 NBA seasons.

But Duke was coming off a five-season run of 62-70, 13-47 in the ACC. Duke went 1-8 in the ACC Tournament from 1970 through 1977. Freshmen had only been eligible for varsity competition since 1973 and a team starting four underclassmen was considered young.

Bill Foster almost had Duke turned around in 1977, his third season at Duke, but an 11-3 start torpedoed into a 14-13 final when senior star Tate Armstrong broke his right wrist.

Spanarkel and Gminski returned from that team. Four newcomers helped push Duke to another level. Banks was the nation's top recruit and he was joined by another freshman forward, Kenny Dennard.

But Duke still had a gaping hole at point guard. Junior Steve Gray had struggled the previous season after Armstrong's injury. He was nudged aside for a pair of transfers.

Durham native John Harrell began his college career across town at North Carolina Central, before transferring to Duke. A cerebral son of a college professor, Harrell was eligible right away.

Bob Bender had transferred from Indiana at the 1976-77 semester break and wasn't eligible until mid-season.

Both were sophomores. Harrell got the starts, but the two played roughly equal amounts.

Duke was unranked at the beginning of the season and didn't hit the polls until mid-January, after a 92-84 win over second-ranked North Carolina moved Duke's record to 12-3.

The win over North Carolina was Duke's first in conference play since 1972 and ended a 1-16 stretch; Duke's win came in the 1974 Big Four Tournament.

This was Duke's first appearance in the polls since late in the 1971 season.

Gminski scored 29 points against the Tar Heels and later recalled "the last few minutes were the loudest sustained noise I've ever heard in Cameron. After the game, we knew we had something going. It was a moment of realization."

The team gradually solidified its many strengths, while minimizing its few weaknesses.

Foster decided to go with a 2-3 zone. "We wanted to play more man-to-man," he told me later, "but the zone defense was going so well we decided to stick with it. It played to our strengths."

Spanarkel set a still-standing school record with 93 steals, while Gminski notched 92 blocks, still the sixth-best mark in Duke history.

The team hit a brief roadblock when Gminski hurt a toe early in a game at Virginia. Duke lost that game and the subsequent game at Wake Forest, which Gminski sat out.

Gminski recovered and Duke went on a five-game winning streak. The Blue Devils traveled to Chapel Hill tied for first place with North Carolina on the regular season's final day.

Duke led much of the game, with Banks, Spanarkel, and Gminski all scoring over 20 points. But it was Phil Ford's final home game, and the National Player of the Year scored a career-high 34 points, as Carolina escaped, 87-83.

A maximum of two teams per conference could make the NCAA Tournament field in 1978. The ACC Tournament winner got the automatic bid, but the regular-season winner earned a de facto bid.

This meant that Duke needed to win the conference tournament or lose in the championship game to North Carolina.

Duke had comfortable wins over Clemson and Maryland to advance to the title game for the first time since 1969.

North Carolina didn't hold up its end of the bargain, losing to Wake Forest in the semifinals.

A Wake Forest win would put Duke in the NIT and the Deacons were good enough to pull it off, with 1977 ACC Player of the Year Rod Griffith and future 10-year NBA player Frank Johnson leading the way.

Wake led early, 42-37 at the half.

"Our immaturity showed up in the first half," Banks said. "We grew up in the second half. We realized where we were and got our dander up."

Duke controlled the second half and won 85-77, with Gminski (25), Banks (22), and Spanarkel (20) providing most of the offense.

Spanarkel was named tournament MVP, but Gminski proved to be the unstoppable force inside, with 38 rebounds in three games.

Duke relied on another strength, converting 55-64 (85.9 percent) from the line.

This was not an aberration. Duke would end up leading the NCAA with a 78.8 percentage from the line, still a school best, including 24-24 against Davidson.

Duke's first NCAA appearance since 1966 was almost a short one. Opening in Charlotte, Duke struggled with Rhode Island's Sly Williams (27 points).

Williams went to the foul line with 17 seconds left and a 62-61 lead. He missed the first end of the bonus before Gminski rebounded and was fouled.

Duke had been uncharacteristically shaky (9-14) from the line. But Gminski calmly knocked down both foul shots and Rhode Island missed twice at the other end.

Duke survived and advanced to Providence to play Ivy League champions Pennsylvania.

For the second time the young Blue Devils had to rely on toughness and poise down the stretch, against a veteran team.

Duke trailed by eight points late, when Gminski blocked shots on three consecutive possessions.

Duke went on a 16-4 run and won 84-80. Philly native Banks had 21 points and 10 rebounds against the hometown team that had so coveted him.

Penn coach Bob Weinhauer called Duke "lumbering elephants" after the game and predicted that Villanova, another Philadelphia school, would run over and around Duke in the next round.

The lumbering elephants jumped to a 21-6 lead over Villanova and never let them back into the game, winning 90-72. Duke's big three combined for 60 points.

Banks again dominated a team from his hometown, barely missing a triple-double, with 17 points, 10 rebounds, and nine assists.

The 1978 Final Four was held in St. Louis, with Duke and Notre Dame meeting in one semifinal, Kentucky and Arkansas in the other.

Digger Phelps had his best team, with seven future NBA players in the rotation.

One of those was future NBA All-Star Bill Laimbeer. But Gminski outscored Laimbeer 29-7.

Duke led 43-29 at the half and had a 16-point lead with about four minutes left. Donald Williams led a furious Irish comeback that made the score 88-86 Duke. But Duke's foul-shooting prowess pulled it out, with Spanarkel and Harrell each hitting four straight down the stretch.

Harrell's final two free throws gave Duke a 90-86 win.

Duke shot 32-37 from the line, with Spanarkel going 12-12.

Kentucky won the other semifinal contest, creating a matchup between two teams that were polar opposites. Four of Kentucky's top six players were seniors, all business.

Duke was young and carefree. Banks and Dennard in particular charmed all with their exuberance.

Kentucky had spent much of the season atop the national polls and they did so on merit.

They led virtually the entire game, including 45-38 at the half. Duke's 2-3 zone had taken them a long way, but Kentucky senior forward Jack "Goose" Givens kept finding holes in the seams and made Duke pay for every lapse. He scored 41 points, bettered in the title game only by UCLA's Bill Walton's 44 points against Memphis in 1973.

Kentucky built its lead to 16. Then it was Duke's turn to mount a furious rally, cutting the deficit to four in the final minute. But the Blue Devils got no closer than that.

The final was 94-88. Banks said Duke "gave them too much respect. It took us most of the game to realize they weren't better than us. We just ran out of time."

Spanarkel added, "They had a little more maturity, a little more polish."

Duke's big three all scored at least 20 points. But Givens shot 18 for 27 from the field, and it's hard to beat anyone when allowing 94 points.

"We were young and naïve and just going along for the ride," Spanarkel told me later. "We thought we had turned it around and [were] going in the right direction. But we certainly weren't thinking Final Four."

18. The Plumlees. Miles and Mason Plumlee played for Duke's 2010 title team and Marshall Plumlee played for the 2015 team. All three Plumlees were key reserves for those title teams and later became starters.

The Plumlees are all around seven feet tall. They all grew up in Indiana but attended Christ School in Arden, North Carolina, not far from Asheville.

All three plied their trade around the basket. The trio combined for four 3-pointers in their Duke careers.

Their father Perky played basketball at Tennessee Tech and mother Leslie played at Purdue. Their maternal grandfather Albert Schultz played basketball at Michigan Tech and on the U.S. Air Force team, while two uncles also played college hoops.

Miles is the oldest, 18 months older than Mason and almost four years older than Marshall.

Yet, Mason was the first one in the Duke truck. He verbally committed to Duke in February 2008, his junior season at Christ School.

Miles had signed with Stanford the previous fall. But he was released from his letter of intent when Stanford head coach Trent Johnson left for LSU.

Miles signed with Duke that spring.

Miles played little as a freshman. But both Plumlees were major contributors to Duke's 2010 title team, concentrating on defense and rebounding, combining for 30 minutes, nine points, eight rebounds, and 1.6 blocks per game.

Miles and Mason had their best college seasons as seniors. Miles averaged over seven rebounds per game in 2012, including a 22-rebound performance against Maryland.

That's the most rebounds by any Duke player under Mike Krzyzewski's tenure.

Mason is the most talented of the trio, the best blend of athleticism and skill. He averaged 11 points and 9 rebounds per game as a junior in 2012, making third-team All-ACC.

Mason could have declared for the NBA following his junior season and been picked late in the first round. But he thought he had things to improve.

For one, he had to improve his foul shooting. Barely a 50 percent foul shooter over his first three seasons, Plumlee improved to a 68 percent shooter in 2013. He refined his low-post moves and averaged 17.1 points per game, with 10 rebounds and 1.4 blocks per game.

Only Shelden Williams (twice) has averaged more rebounds in a season at Duke for Krzyzewski.

Plumlee was first-team All-ACC, second-team All-America, and won the Pete Newell Award as the nation's best big man.

Duke won 30 games in 2013, including three in the NCAA Tournament before losing to eventual champion Louisville in the Elite Eight.

Mason Plumlee set still-standing Duke records with 87 dunks in 2013 and 217 for his career. The high-flying Plumlee spent so much time above the rim that his teammates joked that he needed to wear a helmet for protection.

Marshall joined his brothers for the 2011-12 season, making Duke one of only a handful of college teams to have three brothers. But Marshall was a healthy redshirt that season, meaning he and Miles didn't play in any games together.

Then he broke a foot in practice the following season and played only 50 minutes.

By the time he got healthy, he was backing up elite talents, like Jabari Parker (2014) and Jahlil Okafor (2015). He became a valuable, high-energy contributor off the bench.

He had 10 points and 10 rebounds in Duke's 2015 NCAA opener against Robert Morris and grabbed three rebounds in the Final Four win over Michigan State.

Marshall finally got his shot in 2016, technically as a grad student, when senior Amile Jefferson's season ended after nine games due to a broken foot.

The youngest Plumlee posted seven double-doubles, while averaging 8.3 points, 8.6 rebounds, and 1.6 blocks per game. He averaged 9.8 rebounds per game in ACC play, including a pair of 17-rebound games. Plumlee had a career-high 23 points in an NCAA Tournament win over UNC-Wilmington.

He played more minutes in 2016 (1099) than his first three seasons combined (678).

Mike Krzyzewski praised the brothers as "three really good guys, great players, from a great family, in [our] program. We're blessed to have that. Each one has turned out to be a huge success."

Marshall agrees. "The Duke connection has really spoiled our family. To have such a great support system, being so far from home, it's like a second family."

19. Austin Rivers, in 2012. Rivers led Duke to a 27-7 mark with a team-leading 15.5 points per game, making him the first Duke freshman since Johnny Dawkins in 1983 to lead the team in scoring.

The son of former NBA player and current NBA coach Glenn "Doc" Rivers, Austin arrived at Duke as one of the nation's top recruits. Duke was replacing Nolan Smith, Kyle Singler, and Kyrie Irving from its 2011 team and needed firepower.

Mike Krzyzewski made it clear that Rivers would be responsible for providing that firepower.

"He's our one guy who can cross some help-and-recover situations, get another team in foul trouble, get us to the bonus early," Krzyzewski said early in the season. "He's just got to adjust to the game, but he's strong with the ball."

Rivers agreed. "I'm a scorer. I'm always going to be aggressive."

Rivers scored 527 points in his single season at Duke but will always be remembered for three of those, on February 8, in Chapel Hill.

Duke trailed North Carolina by 13 points in the second half and by 10 with 2:40 remaining.

Duke cut it to a point, 83-82, with 14 seconds left, with North Carolina's Tyler Zeller at the foul line.

Zeller was an 80 percent foul shooter. But he missed the second shot before Mason Plumlee grabbed the rebound and got the ball to Rivers.

Rivers calmly dribbled down court, took advantage of a Plumlee screen, and stared down Zeller. Teammate Seth Curry, about 15 feet away in the corner, screamed at Rivers, "shoot it, shoot it."

Rivers got the shot off over Zeller's outstretched arms. The ball hung in the air before dropping through. The clock read zero and the scoreboard read Duke 85 North Carolina 84.

The 3-pointer was the sixth of the game for Rivers. Curry added four more, with Duke outscoring North Carolina 42-3 from beyond the arc.

Rivers ended with a career-high 29 points.

"I swear the ball was in the air for like 10 minutes," Rivers said following the game. "My heart dropped. I shot it with confidence but when I was walking back it looked good and I was like 'Please go in.' When it went in, my heart jumped. It was the best feeling I've ever had in my life."

Duke's 2012 season fell apart when junior forward Ryan Kelly sprained an ankle in practice, days before the ACC Tournament. Duke lost two of its three postseason games, including its NCAA opener to Lehigh, despite Rivers's 19 points.

In addition to making first-team All-ACC, Rivers was voted ACC Rookie of the Year and third-team All-America by the National Association of Basketball Coaches.

Rivers opted for the NBA draft and was selected as the 10th pick in the draft.

One season, one indelible memory.

20. Art Heyman led Duke to the 1963 Final Four. He was ACC and National Player of the Year, the Final Four Most Outstanding Player, and Duke's leading scorer and rebounder.

Heyman was a 6-foot-5, 205-pound forward, who came to Duke from Long Island. He committed to North Carolina but backed out when his stepfather and North Carolina coach Frank McGuire had a heated argument over Heyman's future role in the program.

Heyman de-committed about the same time as Vic Bubas took over as coach at Duke. Bubas swooped in and wrapped up Heyman within days.

Heyman not only started from day one of his sophomore season (1961), but he was Duke's best player and one of the ACC's best players.

Heyman wasn't a great shooter, but he was a great scorer. He was strong, tough, and fearless. His default mode was to attack the basket at every opportunity. If he missed, there was a good chance he would grab the rebound. He also was a gifted passer. Had assists been an official statistic in those days, he likely would have led Duke.

Heyman was a controversial figure. He was physical and could be quick-tempered, a trait aggravated by years of anti-Semitic taunting from opposing players, coaches, and fans. A fight between Heyman and North Carolina's Larry Brown and Donnie Walsh in a 1961 game has become well publicized.

Heyman delivered a hard foul on Brown late in the game, Brown came up swinging, and the benches emptied for 10 minutes.

Art Heyman and Vic Bubas celebrate a Duke victory. (AP Photo/ William A. Smith)

But Heyman produced on the court at a high level. Heyman was a unanimous first-team All-ACC selection as a sophomore, junior, and senior, an accomplishment matched only by David Thompson (1973–75).

Duke went 69-14 in Heyman's career, 35-7 in ACC regular-season games. Duke was ranked in the AP top-10 every game Heyman played.

But Heyman only played in a single NCAA Tournament.

The sophomore Heyman joined a senior-dominated team that included Carroll Youngkin, Doug Kistler, and Howard Hurt, coming off an Elite Eight season.

Duke was a powerhouse early, starting 16-1. But that 16th win was that North Carolina game with the fight and subsequent suspensions, including a three-game suspension for Heyman

The Blue Devils finished the regular season 10-4 in the ACC and advanced to the ACC Tournament title game, where they lost 96-81 to Wake Forest.

Those seniors left after the 1961 season but were replaced with some talented sophomores, most notably 6-foot-4 forward Jeff Mullins. Heyman and Mullins teamed up for two seasons and might be the most talented duo in Duke history.

Mullins was about the same size as Heyman and about as effective. But he was smooth where Heyman was rugged, controlled where Heyman was spontaneous, and a better shooter, probably more versatile.

Mullins averaged just over 20 points and 10 rebounds in 1962. This remains the only time in Duke history that two players averaged in double figures in rebounds and one of only three times two players averaged over 20 points per game;

Heyman and Mullins replicated the feat the following year and Jim Spanarkel and Mike Gminski did it in 1978.

Duke again had a great regular season, 19-4, but again came up empty in the tournament. Duke turned looking forward to a title rematch with Wake Forest into looking past semifinal opponent Clemson. Clemson beat the Blue Devils in the semifinal 77-72.

Heyman had one final shot at the brass ring and put it all together in 1963, aided immeasurably by Mullins.

Duke lost twice early in December, 72-69 to Davidson and 71-69 to Miami, and then proceeded to blitz the ACC, 14-0. This included a 111-71 demolition of then sixth-ranked West Virginia and ACC Tournament wins by margins of 19, 17, and 11 points.

Heyman had 40 points and 24 rebounds in his home finale, a 106-93 win over North Carolina.

Duke entered the NCAA Tournament on an 18-game winning streak, the longest in school history at the time.

Duke extended that streak with an 81-76 win in the NCAAs over NYU and an impressive 73-59 win over St. Joseph's in the East Region title game. Heyman had 38 points and 23 rebounds in the two games, but Mullins led everyone with 49 points.

These two wins equaled the total of NCAA Tournament wins in school history and sent Duke to its first Final Four.

Louisville was the host. Two-time defending champion Cincinnati was ranked at the top of the AP poll, with Duke at the second spot and Loyola of Chicago ranked third.

Loyola and Duke were matched in one semifinal. The Ramblers likely were the nation's quickest team and Duke struggled with turnovers and transition defense. Loyola led 44-31 at the half.

Heyman led a comeback. Duke trailed 75-72 when Heyman fouled out on a charge. Loyola pulled away after that, winning 94-75.

Heyman had 29 points and 12 rebounds.

Loyola defeated Cincinnati in overtime for the title, while Duke pounded Oregon State 85-63 in the consolation game, with Heyman scoring 22.

Heyman was the first pick of the 1963 NBA draft and played six seasons in the NBA and ABA before retiring, a victim of a bad back and an inability to get along with coaches.

Vic Bubas has always been an advocate for Heyman, who died in 2012.

"Of all the players I coached, he was the one I wanted to get the ball into his hands. If he missed a shot, he would get it back. He had a nose for the basket. I think of all my players he had the best ability to get it to the open man, especially if that man was moving. I had to monitor him closely. He was very explosive. The trick was to direct the fire the right way. Sometimes as a coach you had to take certain measures to keep him on track. He always responded in the right way. I had great respect for him."

Heyman's 25.1 points per game average is the best in Duke history, while his 10.9 rebounds per game ranks fourth. Heyman went to the foul line almost 11 times per game. He was third-team AP All-America in 1961, second-team in 1962, and first-team and AP Player of the Year in 1963.

"I helped start it," Heyman told me. "I went to hospitals. I never said no. I was a good student, got a degree in history. I'm not as bad as people think I am."

21. Ryan Kelly came back from a foot injury on March 2, 2013, hitting 10 of 14 from the field, 7 of 9 from 3-point range, and 9 of 12 from the line. Kelly accomplished this feat after one practice, leading Duke to a 79-76 victory over fifth-ranked Miami.

Ryan Kelly's father Chris played basketball at Yale and his mother Doreen played volleyball at Pennsylvania. Two Ivy League–educated athletes as parents gave Kelly a head start in the academic-athletic sweepstakes, and he made abundant use of it. He was an honor roll student at Raleigh's prestigious Ravenscroft Academy—where his mother is headmistress—and a McDonald's All-American on the hardcourt.

The 6-foot-11 Kelly played 227 minutes on Duke's 2010 NCAA title team but became a rotation player as a sophomore.

Kelly averaged 12 points and five rebounds per game in 2012 but missed the postseason with an injured foot. The highlight of that season came in Hawaii's Maui Classic, where he was named MVP after leading Duke to three wins, with 51 points.

There was also a game in Atlanta when Kelly hit all 14 free throws, most in the final minutes, as Duke edged Georgia Tech 81-74.

Kelly entered his senior season poised for big things.

"Ryan is one of the most underrated players not just in the ACC but in the entire country," assistant coach Steve Wojciechowski said at the beginning of the season.

Mike Krzyzewski called Kelly the "prototypical stretch 4," a name for a power forward who can shoot from the outside at a high level. Kelly was Duke's best defensive communicator and a reliable ball-handler and foul shooter.

He held Kentucky's Kyle Wiltjer to five points in a 75-68 win, scored 15 points in a 73-68 win over fourth-ranked Ohio State, and notched 22 points in a win over Wake Forest.

This all came crashing down on the night of January 8 against Clemson, when Kelly went up for a shot and landed wrong.

He would miss 13 games and Duke would lose four of them, all of them in the ACC.

Kelly elected to delay surgery until the offseason and maintained some conditioning on Duke's underwater treadmill.

He practiced a single time before going out to face a talented and physical Miami squad.

By any rational standards, he should have struggled with conditioning, timing, and rhythm.

Instead, he scored 20 points in just the first half, including seven of Duke's first nine points. He hit a 3-pointer to put Duke up 58-56 with nine minutes left.

Mike Krzyzewski called Kelly's performance "one for the ages. Probably as good a performance as any Duke player has had at Cameron."

Kelly's thoughts?

"I just knew I was going to play my hardest. Honestly, though, more than anything it was just going to be whether I could hold up with my breathing. I haven't played any games in a long time, and being in a game is a lot different from being in practice or anything you can do. When something so special to you is taken away, you want it even more."

Kelly acknowledges that he played that game on an adrenaline high that he was unable to duplicate after that.

Duke advanced to the Elite Eight, where they lost to Louisville.

Kelly scored seven points in that loss and ended his season averaging 13 points and five rebounds per game.

22. Duke's Jahlil Okafor, in 2015. The 6-foot-11 post player had the best freshman season in Duke history. He led Duke with 17.3 points, 8.5 rebounds, and 1.4 blocks per game, while shooting 66.4 percent from the field, the third best mark in school history.

Okafor was considered the nation's best prepster at Whitney M. Young Magnet School in Chicago.

He arrived at Duke as something of a throwback, a refined back-to-the-basket, low-post scorer. He did not attempt a single 3-pointer at Duke. But he had 64 dunks, the second-highest total in Duke history.

Mike Krzyzewski made it clear from the beginning that he had high expectations for Okafor.

"He is a dominant player," Krzyzewski said after Duke's public intra-squad game. "Jahlil, he just makes shots. He has a great feel for the game."

Okafor lived up to the hype. He was named ACC Freshman of the Week the first three weeks of the season. He scored 17 points in his third game, a win over Michigan State.

Okafor had 25 points and 20 rebounds against Elon in his ninth game, on his 19th birthday, the first Duke freshman to have a 20-rebound game.

ACC competition didn't slow him down. He had 28 points against Boston College, his first conference foe, as well as 42 points and 27 rebounds in two games against Notre Dame.

He also proved his toughness in an overtime win over North Carolina, rolling an ankle in the first half but returning to play 41 minutes.

Krzyzewski called it a "gutty performance. For any kid you worry, but he's special. I was shocked that he wanted to come back in during the first half. Just mentally for him to get over it right then."

Okafor led everyone with 13 rebounds and downplayed the significance of the injury, citing "a lot of good emotions."

It was serious enough for him to sit out one game and miss some practices down the stretch. But he returned after one game to key Duke to a come-from-behind road win against Virginia Tech with 30 points.

Duke opened its NCAA Tournament play in Charlotte and Okafor had 47 points as Duke handled Robert Morris and San Diego State. He didn't score much in Duke's wins over Utah and Gonzaga but grabbed eight rebounds in each game.

Okafor scored 18 points as Duke defeated Michigan State 81-61 in the Final Four.

Foul trouble held him to 22 minutes in Duke's title win over Wisconsin. But he came off the bench late and hit two huge field goals as Duke overcame a nine-point deficit.

Tyus Jones talked about Okafor's contributions following the game.

"We didn't have to say anything to Jah. He's all about the team. . . . He got into some foul trouble, but he was able to come back in. Because of his positive attitude, he made some big plays for us down the stretch."

He was a unanimous pick for ACC Freshman of the Year, unanimous pick for first-team All-ACC, and received 44 of the 64 votes cast for ACC Player of the Year. He made every first-team All-America squad, was voted National Freshman of the Year, and was runner-up to Wisconsin's Frank Kaminsky for the National Player of the Year awards.

Okafor left for the NBA after his one season at Duke. The Philadelphia 76ers picked him third in the draft and he averaged 17.5 points per game in his rookie season.

23. Gene Banks, in 1977. Banks was a member of the first McDonald's All-America team. He went on to an All-America career at Duke.

This wasn't the first attempt to honor high school basketball players. *Parade Magazine* began presenting its All-America teams in 1957 and continues to this day.

But the McDonald's team has the backing of one of the world's most successful businesses and has a nationally televised showcase game. Being named a McDonald's All-America player is seen as validation of prep stardom.

Banks is arguably the most important recruit in Duke basketball history, for two reasons.

The first is timing. Banks was a legend at West Philadelphia High School. A rare blend of power, skill, and grace, Banks was given the nickname "Tinkerbell" due to his ability to fly through the air.

Banks and New York City's Albert King were considered the nation's top two high school players, ranked just above Michigan prospect Earvin "Magic" Johnson.

By the middle of his senior season Banks had narrowed his choices to UCLA, Notre Dame, North Carolina, Pennsylvania, and Duke.

UCLA was only two years removed from John Wooden's last NCAA title. Dean Smith and UNC were perennial powers and Digger Phelps was moving Notre Dame in a similar path. Penn was the local choice but also a top program, good enough to make the 1979 Final Four.

Then there was Duke, a fading program, seemingly living on past glories.

Banks thought otherwise. He got along with Duke coach Bill Foster. He recognized that Duke had top-level talent already in place, enough that he could help put them over the top.

"I had a great visit," Banks told me years later. "What really sold me was the people. The whole Duke community. I thought I could help make them a national power. People thought I was crazy."

Banks took a leap of faith.

Gene Banks was the first high-profile, inner-city African American basketball player to play for Duke.

Duke only had one active black player in 1977, when Banks committed—forward Harold Morrison; John Harrell was sitting out his transfer year. Four of the first six black players Duke recruited transferred before completing their eligibility.

Banks helped change Duke's preppy reputation. He was a great talent on the court, but also a charismatic and popular figure off the court.

Banks made an immediate impact. He was the most talented of five newcomers who joined holdovers Jim Spanarkel and Mike Gminski in transforming Duke from pretender to contender. Banks scored 14 points in his first game, 18 in his second.

He wasn't the best player on that team. Spanarkel and Gminski scored more points, and Gminski grabbed more rebounds. Both were first-team All-ACC; Banks was second-team.

But the 6-foot-8, 220-pound Banks may have been the most versatile, averaging 17 points, eight rebounds, and four assists per game, blending a dominating physical presence and a palpable joy in playing basketball.

Banks excelled in the NCAA Tournament, tallying 96 points in five tournament games, including 22 in the title game, a 94-88 loss to Kentucky, playing through a death threat that had been called in to a St. Louis television station before the game.

That 1978 season promised so much and in some sense, Banks's career peaked that year. Unlike Johnson or even King, who became ACC Player of the Year at Maryland in 1980, Banks never refined his game, never developed a consistent jump shot or point-guard skills. He never again played in a Final Four.

But that's an overly harsh assessment. Banks maintained his status as a second-team All-ACC player in 1979 and 1980. He continued to score in the mid-teens and average around eight rebounds per game. A thunderous dunk over Virginia's 7-foot-4 Ralph Sampson in 1980 still inspires awe. Banks averaged 20 points per game as Duke won the 1980 ACC Tournament.

Foster left Duke after that 1980 season, replaced by Mike Krzyzewski, much younger than Foster and more intense. It took some time for Banks and Krzyzewski to get on the same page, but they did, and Banks went out on a high note, leading the ACC with 18.5 points per game and making first-team All-ACC for the only time in his career.

Banks's final regular-season home game was against a North Carolina team that would make it all the way to the NCAA title game, where they lost to Indiana.

Banks handed out roses to the student body before the game and backed it up on the court. He hit a long jumper at the buzzer to send it to overtime and converted an offensive rebound late in the extra period for a 66-65 win.

He scored 25 points, with seven rebounds.

Banks was back in Cameron two weeks later, as Duke hosted an NIT game against North Carolina A&T. He tried to draw a charge early in the game, fell, and broke his right wrist.

His Duke career was over—on the court, that is. Banks defied the skeptics by not only graduating on time but delivering a commencement speech.

Banks played six seasons in the NBA before an Achilles injury ended his days in the league. He scored 2,079 points at Duke, tied with Jason Williams for eighth place. He's ninth in career rebounds and was the first Duke player to be named All-ACC four times.

24. Jabari Parker led Duke with 19.1 points and 8.7 rebounds per game in 2014. The 6-foot-8 post player also led Duke with 1.2 blocks per game. The ACC and National Freshman of the Year, Parker was consensus first-team All-America and runner-up for ACC Player of the Year. His scoring average is the best ever for a Duke freshman.

Parker's father Sonny played six seasons in the NBA and taught the fundamentals to his son, who arrived at Duke with a varied and advanced skill set.

He scored 22 in his first game at Duke, a 34-point win over Davidson, after which he described his role on the team: "Coach is just putting me everywhere on the floor, not having a primary position. With the structure of our offense, I get to go inside-out and that's what I'm comfortable with."

The personable Chicago native led Duke with 61 dunks, went to the foul line 214 times, and made 38 3-pointers, indications of his versatile repertoire.

The 2014 season did not end well for Duke, which lost its tournament opener to Mercer. But the team did win 26 games, including victories over UCLA, Michigan, and Virginia.

The team's most memorable victory was a 66-60 win over top-ranked Syracuse. Parker led Duke with 19 points and 10 rebounds and made all three of his 3-pointers against Syracuse's fabled zone.

Krzyzewski praised Parker's game.

"I thought he started out young in the game, and got old real quick. The last 25 minutes he was a real man."

Parker's last home game was against North Carolina. He scored 30 points in leading Duke to a 93-81 win. It is the most points ever scored by a Duke freshman in a Duke-Carolina game.

Parker scored 61 points in three ACC Tournament games, including 23 in the championship-game loss to Virginia.

Duke entered the NCAA Tournament seeded third in the Midwest and ranked eighth nationally. But Parker and sophomore Rodney Hood picked a bad afternoon to turn cold at the same time; they shot a combined six for 24 in Duke's loss.

Prior to Parker, Johnny Dawkins (1983) and Austin Rivers (2012) led Duke in scoring as freshmen, while Mike Gminski (1977) was the first of six freshmen to lead in rebounding.

Freshman Jahlil Okafor led Duke in scoring and rebounding the following season.

25. The final minute of Duke's January 27, 2001 game at Maryland is known as the "Miracle Minute." Duke trailed Maryland by 12 points with barely a minute left, sent the game into overtime, and pulled out the victory.

Duke and Maryland had a pretty intense rivalry for about a decade.

The competition was never fiercer than it was in 2001. Duke began the season ranked second in the AP poll, Maryland fifth. They were first and fourth in the final AP poll. Both teams had five future NBA players.

Nate James was a Maryland native who elected to play for Duke.

"The games had a different tone to them," he told me later. "They were nastier games, pretty heated. Gary Williams's teams took after him, tough and tenacious."

The first meeting of the season remains arguably the most famous regular-season game in Duke history.

Maryland used a 20-4 run to open up a 44-29 lead late in the first half.

Duke closed on an 8-2 run to stay in contact, and remained down at intermission, 46-37.

The teams traded baskets most of the second half; Maryland was unable to put Duke away, but also Duke was unable to catch up.

Duke's Jason Williams was the nation's best guard. But he struggled against Steve Blake, his Maryland counterpart.

"I had a horrible game," Williams recalled. "I was lathered up three days before the game. I had heard all the stuff about Steve Blake being a Williams-buster. Sometimes you want it so bad, that you hurt yourself. [Blake] had a long wingspan. He was hard to get around."

Duke kept on attacking and forced Blake into his fifth foul, with two minutes left.

He was replaced by Drew Nicholas, who went on to have one of the worst minutes imaginable.

Still, it was 89-77, with 65 seconds left and chants of "overrated" filling Cole Field House.

James hit a 3-pointer. Nicholas made one of two from the line.

Williams hit a layup with 53.5 seconds left, making it 90-82.

"I told Cdu [Chris Duhon] that we could funnel Nicholas into the corner," Williams said. "We had to make something happen."

Williams got a steal and hit a 3-pointer. It was 90-85. "When you see a little blood, take a bigger bite," Williams said. "Once we saw them look a little defeated, we had them exactly where we wanted them."

Duke fouled Nicholas, who missed both foul shots. Williams hit a 3 and it was 90-88; no longer was anybody chanting "overrated."

Maryland still had the ball and the lead, but the team was clearly rattled. James stole an inbounds pass and got it to Dunleavy, who missed a 3.

James crashed the boards and barely missed a tip-in but drew a foul.

"I was upset because I should have won the game," James remembered. "I had a tip that went in and out. It should have been a 3-point play. Once that didn't happen, I told myself to clear your mind, the only thing that matters is these free throws. Once I did that, to silence the crowd, it was a great feeling. Once we did that, I knew it was our game."

Maryland had the final shot, but Nicholas missed.

Overtime.

Williams and James had spurred the comeback, but Shane Battier ruled the overtime. Battier scored Duke's last six points and blocked a last-second Juan Dixon shot to preserve a 98-96 win.

Krzyzewski praised Williams for the comeback.

"In the last minute, Jason showed who he was at both ends of the floor. When he got on a roll, he was awfully hard to stop."

James added, "Never leave the game with bullets in your gun. We rose to the occasion, guys stepped up and made big plays. We drew on that in the Final Four. When you've done it once, you know you can do it again."

Duke went on to play Maryland three more times that season. Maryland won in Cameron after Carlos Boozer broke his right foot during the game.

Duke prevailed despite an 11-point deficit to defeat Maryland 84-82 in the ACC Tournament and overcame a 39-17 Maryland lead to defeat the Terps in the Final Four on the way to the school's third NCAA title.

This is the only time a Mike Krzyzewski–coached Duke team had played an opponent four times in the same season.

26. The 1999 Duke team. Elton Brand was the first pick and was followed by Trajan Langdon (11), Corey Maggette (13), and William Avery (14).

Langdon was the only senior. Brand and Avery left Duke after their sophomore seasons, while Maggette departed after his freshman season. They were the first Duke players to declare for the NBA draft with eligibility remaining.

Brand was a two-time NBA All-Star and Maggette played 14 seasons in the NBA. Langdon and Avery had lesser NBA stints but had long careers overseas.

Through the 2015-16 season, Duke has had 39 first-round picks.

27. Doug Gottlieb made that comment during ESPN's broadcast of the Duke–Arizona State game November 25, 2009. A little over four months later, that alarmingly un-athletic team won Duke's fourth NCAA title.

Duke entered the season coming off a 2009 ACC Tournament title and a Sweet Sixteen appearance. But Gerald Henderson not surprisingly opted for the NBA after his junior season, promising freshman Elliott Williams surprisingly transferred back home to Memphis, and Lithuanian Marty Pocius gave up a redshirt-senior season to start a pro career in his home country.

Henderson, Williams, and Pocius were all athletic, mid-sized wings and only one of Duke's three incoming freshmen—Andre Dawkins—fit that mold. Classmates Mason Plumlee and Ryan Kelly were 6-foot-10 and 6-foot-9.

But Mason Plumlee and older brother Miles were two of the most athletic big men in the country, a nuance apparently lost on Gottlieb, an ESPN analyst.

Gottlieb's comments were made before an NIT preseason tip-off game, which Duke won 64-53. Duke won the championship two days later, defeating Connecticut 68-59.

Krzyzewski was asked about the comments following the Connecticut win. "He should be an expert on alarmingly non-athletic," Krzyzewski sarcastically responded. "So I'll have to take a look at that a little bit closer because it comes from an expert who actually knows what it feels like to be alarmingly non-athletic. . . . And I would rather not get into a discussion with Doug because I have respect of his stature and he should have his arguments with people of similar stature."

"Alarmingly un-athletic" became a team punch line.

Duke returned six players from its 2009 ACC Tournament championship team, most notably its perimeter trio of Jon Scheyer, Kyle Singler, and Nolan Smith.

Scheyer was a heady and versatile 6-foot-5 senior. His move from shooting guard to point guard in mid-season jump-started Duke's 2009 stretch run.

Singler was a 6-foot-8 junior forward, tough-as-nails but with considerable perimeter skills.

Scheyer and Singler were both first-team All-ACC in 2010 and Scheyer was a consensus second-team All-America selection.

But Smith made the greatest improvement, overcoming the injuries that had hampered him earlier in his career. The 6-foot-2 junior was Duke's best perimeter defender and an aggressive attacker.

The trio combined for 53 points and 10 assists per game.

Duke rotated the Plumlee brothers, 7-foot-0 senior Brian Zoubek, and 6-foot-8 senior defensive specialist Lance Thomas at the two interior spots.

Duke began the season ranked ninth in the AP poll, started 13-1, and never dropped out of the top 10.

Krzyzewski made a crucial lineup change in mid-February. Duke had been starting Miles Plumlee and Thomas, while bringing Zoubek and Mason Plumlee off the bench. Thomas strained a knee in Duke's 64-54 win at Chapel Hill.

It wasn't clear if Thomas would be able to play the next game against Maryland, and Krzyzewski planned to start Zoubek with Mason Plumlee, rather than start both Plumlees (a sophomore and a freshman).

It turned out that Thomas was able to play. But the real story was Zoubek grabbing a career-high 17 rebounds—eight on the offensive end—in Duke's 77-56 win.

Zoubek had been bothered by foot injuries for much of his career.

"This was definitely a matchup [against Maryland] that I wouldn't have played in the past years," he said. "They would've spread it out a little bit. It just proves that my footwork has gotten a lot better and I can handle it. I'm just happy to be able to be out there on the court. I've gotten some extra running in and my legs are a little stronger. In the past, I could get up [to the rim], I was just too tired once I ran down the court."

Zoubek proved to be the missing link. He stayed in the starting lineup (with Thomas) and was the nation's best offensive rebounder down the stretch.

Duke tied Maryland for the ACC regular-season title and handled Virginia, Miami, and Georgia Tech to win the conference tournament.

Duke opened the NCAAs with wins over Arkansas Pine Bluff, California, and Purdue, all by double digits.

Baylor was next, the kind of athletic team that Duke wasn't supposed to be able to handle.

And it certainly wasn't easy. Smith had the best game of his career to that point—finishing with 29 points—and Scheyer added 20 points (five 3-pointers) and five rebounds. But the game was played in Houston in front of almost 50,000 Baylor fans, Singler missed all 10 of his field goal attempts, and Duke trailed most of the second half.

The unsung Thomas made the game's biggest play, digging out a rebound and finding Smith for a 3-pointer that broke a 61-61 tie with 3:32 left. Scheyer followed with another 3-pointer and Duke held on for a 78-71 win.

"Those two 3s in a row, by Nolan and then Jon, those were big-time plays," Krzyzewski said after the game. "The big guys kicked it out and those are the best 3s to take."

Duke was joined in Indianapolis by West Virginia, Butler, and Michigan State.

Duke met sixth-ranked West Virginia and shut down the Mountaineers' high-powered offense in a 78-57 win. Duke held West Virginia to 41 percent shooting, while Singler found his shooting touch, scoring 21 to go along with Scheyer's 23 points, Smith's 19 points, and Zoubek's 10 rebounds.

Duke never trailed after an early 4-2 deficit.

Butler upset Michigan State in the other semifinal, and again Duke faced a large, hostile crowd, 70,000 worth.

The 2010 Duke team was not an offensive juggernaut; only the big three averaged more than Zoubek's 5.6 points per game. But Duke surrendered only 61 points per game—Duke's lowest of the shot clock era—to opponents while allowing 40 percent shooting.

Duke had to use all of these resources to escape Butler, in a tough, half-court slugfest, with five ties and 15 lead changes. The teams combined for under 40 percent shooting and made 11 of 35 from beyond the arc—almost all contested. Rebounds were even, and Duke had four more turnovers. Butler's biggest lead was two points, while Duke's was six.

Singler put Duke up 58-55, with 4:47 left. But it would be Duke's last field goal.

Butler had the ball down 60-59. Their star forward Gordon Hayward missed a jumper with Zoubek's hand in his face and Zoubek grabbed his 10th rebound, with 3.6 seconds left.

He made the first foul shot and—per Krzyzewski's instructions—missed the second one, as Butler was out of timeouts. Hayward drew iron on a 60-footer and the final was 61-59.

Singler led everyone with 19 points and was named Final Four Most Outstanding Player.

2

MID-RANGE JUMPER LEVEL

1. Who was the first person to both play in and coach in a Final Four? *Answer on page 95.*

2. Who did Mike Krzyzewski call "our most valuable guy" on Duke's 2015 team? *Answer on page 98.*

3. What is the longest winning streak in Duke history? *Answer on page 104.*

4. Which program has won the most consecutive ACC Tournaments? *Answer on page 109.*

5. What was the first men's college basketball team to win 37 games? *Answer on page 111.*

6. When did Duke first make the NCAA title game? *Answer on page 116.*

7. What is the lowest-scoring game in ACC history? *Answer on page 120.*

8. Who has the highest rebound average in Duke history? *Answer on page 122.*

9. What was the first Duke team ranked No. 1 in the AP poll? *Answer on page 124.*

10. Who holds the Duke and ACC single-game scoring records? *Answer on page 129.*

11. Which team was both the first Duke squad to capture an ACC Tournament and the first Duke team to win an NCAA Tournament game? *Answer on page 131.*

12. Who was the first Duke player to score more than 2,000 career points? *Answer on page 135.*

13. Who is Duke's career leader in steals? *Answer on page 140.*

14. Which Duke player went from a single-digit scorer to ACC Player of the Year in a single season? *Answer on page 140.*

15. Who was the first Duke player to be named National Player of the Year? *Answer on page 141.*

16. Who is the Duke coach who also was head coach at five other schools? *Answer on page 146.*

17. Who made the greatest single-season scoring improvement in ACC history? *Answer on page 149.*

18. What is the greatest individual defensive performance in Duke history? *Answer on page 151.*

19. What is the fewest number of points allowed by Duke in a half in an ACC game? *Answer on page 152.*

20. Which Blue Devil played an entire season with a stress fracture and still made All-America? *Answer on page 155.*

21. Who is Wojo? *Answer on page 158.*

22. Which father and son duo combined to play on six Final Four teams at Duke? *Answer on page 158.*

23. Who is the only player to lead Duke in scoring, rebounding, and assists over an entire season? *Answer on page 162.*

24. Who was the first National Defensive Player of the Year? *Answer on page 165.*

25. Name the Duke player who followed in the footsteps of his father by winning a national title? *Answer on page 167.*

26. Who was the first Duke player to lead the ACC in rebounding? *Answer on page 168.*

27. Who played the most minutes in a Duke uniform? *Answer on page 170.*

MID-RANGE JUMPER – ANSWERS

1. Vic Bubas played for NC State and coached Duke to three Final Fours, participating in the deepest NCAA Tournament advancement by both schools at the time.

Bubas was a native of Gary, Indiana and came south to play for North Carolina State, one of Everett Case's "Hoosier Hotshots."

Bubas wanted to be a college basketball coach and thought Case the person best qualified to help him achieve that goal.

But Bubas was a pretty good college player too. Around 6-foot-2, he was never much of a scorer. But he was a gifted passer and tenacious defender.

NC State won the Southern Conference and received an NCAA bid in 1950, Bubas's junior season.

The NCAA Tournament consisted of eight teams that year.

State was matched against Holy Cross and their star guard, Bob Cousy. Bubas spent much of the game shadowing Cousy and hounded him into an 11 for 38 shooting nightmare.

State won 97-74 and joined CCNY, Baylor, and Bradley in the national semifinals (it wasn't called The Final Four in those days, but it was, for all intents and purposes, the final four).

CCNY edged the Wolfpack 78-73 and then defeated Bradley for the title. NC State defeated Baylor in the consolation game.

Duke star Dick Groat went up against Bubas many times. "Vic defended me as well as anybody," Groat said many years later. "Nobody outworked him and he was always prepared."

State made it back to the NCAAs the next year. But Bubas and fellow seniors Sammy Ranzino and Paul Horvath were ruled ineligible for the tournament due to a rule that banned seniors who had played varsity ball as freshmen. Five of the tournament's 16 teams lost players due to that rule.

Bubas became a State assistant immediately after graduation. He and Case were so close that players referred to them as "Pete and Repeat."

He appeared to be Case's heir apparent.

But Case didn't seem to be going anywhere soon and the Duke job opened up when Harold Bradley left Duke for Texas in the spring of 1959. Bubas actually took a base pay cut to come to Duke, accepting the offer after Duke agreed to let him make up the difference by hosting summer camps on campus.

Bubas turned Duke from a regional power to a national power. Duke won four of the first seven ACC Tournaments under his tutelage. Duke had never won an NCAA Tournament game before Bubas took over but won two in his first season in Durham. Duke won 213 games in the 1960s, trailing only UCLA and Cincinnati for the most in that decade.

Basketball recruiting in the 1950s tended to be regional recruiting of seniors. North Carolina's Frank McGuire almost exclusively recruited his home area, Greater New York City. Case loved kids from the Midwest. Duke and Wake Forest trolled the East Coast, especially Pennsylvania.

Bubas cast his net wider. Bubas brought in players from places such as Texas, Kansas, Illinois, and Montana.

Bubas was the first to start evaluating and recruiting juniors. Dean Smith said that Bubas "taught us all how to recruit."

Duke center Jay Buckley was a superb science student. When asked if he wanted to be the first person on the moon,

Vic Bubas instructs Jeff Mullins and teammates in a 1964 timeout. (AP Photo)

Buckley quipped that he would find Bubas already there, looking for recruits.

Bubas was often called college basketball's first CEO. He was smart, analytical, and focused. He wanted his assistant coaches to be head coaches in waiting and gave them the responsibilities they needed to grow.

He had five assistant coaches at Duke—Fred Shabel, Bucky Waters, Chuck Daly, Tom Carmody, and Hubie Brown. All five became head coaches after leaving Duke. Daly and Brown are in the Naismith Memorial Basketball Hall of Fame.

"His greatest gift was his ability to get the best out of everybody," Waters said well after his coaching career had ended. "Bubas allowed you to grow. He wanted you to expand."

Bubas got tired of recruiting, wanted to do something else. He retired from coaching after the 1969 season, with a record of 213-67, which included a 22-6 mark in the ACC Tournament and an 8-4 mark in the NCAAs. His .768 (106-32) winning percentage in ACC games is the best in conference history.

He was only 42 at the time of his retirement from coaching.

"The thought of getting on another plane and chasing another high school kid was overwhelming," Bubas told me years later.

He became an administrator at Duke before leaving in 1976 to become the first commissioner of the Sunbelt Conference, a position he held through 1990. As a member of the NCAA Basketball Committee, he pushed successfully for the expansion of the NCAA Tournament, shot clocks, and a 3-point shot.

Gene Corrigan, who served on the NCAA Selection Committee with Bubas when Corrigan was the athletic director at Notre Dame, sang Bubas's praises. "Vic was never pushy with his intelligence," he said. "He spoke quietly and eloquently. He was so totally fair in everything. His only agenda was to get it right."

2. Krzyzewski made this comment about senior guard Quinn Cook after a close road win against Florida State. Cook didn't even make first-team All-ACC and wasn't one of the three Duke players selected in the first round of the 2015 NBA draft. In fact, he wasn't drafted at all.

Cook was part of a marvelous group that year that included center Jahlil Okafor—the only freshman to ever be voted ACC Player of the Year—and point guard Tyus Jones—the only ACC freshman to ever be Final Four Most Outstanding Player. The two other freshmen on the squad—forward Justise Winslow and super-sub Grayson Allen—joined Jones on the All Final Four team.

The four freshmen scored 57 percent of Duke's points that season, grabbed 52 percent of the rebounds, and compiled 62 percent of the assists.

Though it's easy to frame Duke's 2015 NCAA title around the freshmen, Cook was the glue that kept everything intact.

Yet it wasn't always smooth for Cook. He didn't play much as a freshman, but seemed to bounce back at the beginning of his sophomore year, during which he was named MVP of the early-season Battle for Atlantis in the Bahamas. Nevertheless, he slumped later that season and rode the performance roller-coaster as a junior, a frustrating blend of raw talent and immaturity, by his own admission prone to dwelling on his mistakes and bringing his team down with bad body language.

He was a point guard, leading Duke in assists in 2013 and 2014.

Krzyzewski brought in highly-touted Tyus Jones, as pure a point guard as pure can be, for the 2014-15 season. Jones had played summer AAU and international ball with the even more highly-touted Okafor. They had a connection rare for freshmen.

Jones was going to start at Cook's old spot.

Cook, in turn, moved to shooting guard—a position he had never played before—and he also embraced the roles of team leader and tutor.

"I'm the senior," Cook said during the 2014-15 season. "I've been here so I know what Coach wants. I can still see things, even when I'm not at the top of the offense, so I want to help Tyus out. He's still learning things on the run, so I just want to help him."

Krzyzewski agreed. "He's doing a great job of leading. His personality is so good right now with these young guys. They love him and he's given them positive stuff."

Cook also became a primary scoring option, contributing 19 points in an 81-71 win over Michigan State and 34 points in two games to win the Coaches Versus Cancer Classic.

Duke took a young team into the hostile environment of Madison, Wisconsin, and stunned second-ranked Wisconsin 81-71, with Tyus Jones scoring 22.

Three uber-talented freshmen, the high-level play of Cook, and solid contributions from role players Amile Jefferson, Matt Jones (no relation to Tyus), and Rasheed Sulaimon led the team to a 14-0 start.

What could go wrong?

Plenty, it turns out. Unable to break into the rotation, reserve forward Semi Ojeleye transferred at the semester break.

Then Duke forgot how to play man-to-man defense, getting torched in back-to-back losses, 87-75 at NC State and even more disturbingly at home, 90-74 to Miami, the first home loss for everyone on the team except Cook.

Making the loss even worse, Winslow suffered a rib injury that would slow him down for weeks.

Four of the next five games were on the road, three against top-10 teams.

It could easily have unraveled.

Krzyzewski went to his bag of tricks and Duke started mixing zone defenses into his trademark man-to-man. Duke stunned Louisville 63-52, upset second-ranked Virginia 69-63—Cook had three 3-pointers—and gave Krzyzewski his 1,000th win with a victory over St. John's.

The trip to South Bend did not end well. Duke gave up a late lead from the foul line—where they went 10 for 20 during the game—and lost to Notre Dame.

But Duke had lost games from the foul line before. What happened after was unprecedented. Krzyzewski dismissed Sulaimon—a valuable 6-foot-4 junior—from the squad for conduct deemed detrimental to the team.

This was the first time Krzyzewski, by then in his 35th year as Duke coach, had ever dismissed a player.

Duke was down to eight recruited players. Practices were scaled back, especially after Okafor rolled an ankle in an over-time win over North Carolina.

But the wins kept on coming. Okafor only missed a game, Winslow got healthy, and Cook maintained his new-found status as 3-point ace.

Cook's best game was at Florida State, where he hit four 3-pointers and scored 26 points, to help Duke overcome a scoreless first six minutes.

It was after this game that Krzyzewski praised Cook.

"He has not only been a good player, a really good player, but he's been a great leader. And our guys follow him. He has been one of my better leaders that I have had at Duke. Of all the guys, I'm most proud of him." Duke finished the regular season winning 14 of 15.

The ACC Tournament showed both how good Duke could be if it stayed focused and how difficult it is to keep a young team focused.

Duke toyed with NC State in the quarterfinals, leading 49-22 at the half, en route to a 77-53 win.

The next night Duke came out flat and uninspired against Notre Dame, digging itself into an early hole, trailing 41-26 at halftime. The Blue Devils never caught up.

Cook had a miserable game, shooting two for 12 and scoring only seven points.

There would be no more slipups.

Duke cruised in Charlotte, 85-56 over Robert Morris and 68-49 over San Diego State. Cook had 22 in the opener and Okafor 26 in the second win.

Duke played Utah in the Sweet Sixteen. Cook failed to hit a 3-pointer for the first time in 46 games and Okafor was held to six points.

But Duke had developed more ways to beat good teams.

Winslow had emerged as one of the nation's top talents. The 6-foot-6, 220-pounder was comfortable inside and out, in half-court and transition, and on offense and defense. His 21 points, 10 rebounds, and two blocks keyed Duke to a 63-57 win over Utah.

Tyus Jones added 15 points.

"He gave us his trust and just believed in us," Winslow said of Krzyzewski. "When you have that, you play like yourself."

Gonzaga was next. This time it was Matt Jones who stepped up, hitting four 3-pointers and leading Duke with 16 points in a 66-52 win.

Duke faced Michigan State in the Final Four, a rematch of an earlier Duke win in Indianapolis, the same town as the 2015 Final Four, albeit different venues.

Duke fell behind 14-6 before exploding, outscoring the Spartans 75-47 after that point, for an 81-61 win. Winslow, Okafor, and Cook led Duke with 19, 18, and 17 points respectively.

Losing coach Tom Izzo jumped on the Cook bandwagon. "My MVP of that team is Cook," Izzo said before the game. "I just think he has everything. He's been through the wars, you know. He's been through some disappointments. I think that makes you a better person."

Duke unleashed another lethal weapon in the game. Grayson Allen was the largely forgotten fourth member of that freshman class.

But he had worked hard in practice and bided his time. Teammate Amile Jefferson said that Allen was a "monster" in practice.

Now, he was a monster in games. He scored nine points in 17 minutes off the bench against Michigan State.

The third-ranked Wisconsin Badgers were the last obstacle. They had been in the Final Four in 2014 and were led by 6-foot-11 Frank Kaminsky, the consensus National Player of the Year.

Duke had defeated Wisconsin earlier in the season, but the two teams had changed so much in the four months since that there wasn't much carryover.

Okafor and Cook had been Duke's two best players. Duke didn't get a lot from either in the title game but still had enough to overcome a nine-point second-half deficit.

Foul trouble held Okafor to 22 minutes, while Cook could only muster six points, all in the first half.

But Jefferson came off the bench for Okafor and grabbed seven big rebounds, while fighting the bigger Kaminsky inside.

Tyus Jones, Winslow, and Allen were the keys. Winslow stuffed the stat sheet with 11 points, nine rebounds, three blocks, and a steal.

Allen came into the game averaging four points per game but gave Duke 16 in 21 minutes, jumpstarting Duke's comeback with several floor-burning loose-ball victories and scoring eight straight points when Duke was on the ropes.

"When we got nine points down, we were in foul trouble and a little bit disjointed," Krzyzewski said after the game. "Grayson put us on his back."

Okafor came off the bench and scored two big baskets.

Tyus Jones delivered the biggest blows, a pair of 3-pointers in the final minutes, the latter giving Duke an eight-point lead with 1:22 left.

The final was 68-63.

Jones led everyone with 23 points and was named Most Outstanding Player of the Final Four.

The four freshmen scored 60 of Duke's 68 points and grabbed 19 of the 33 rebounds.

"My team had great grit and determination," Krzyzewski noted. "Our defense down the stretch was magnificent."

"Surreal," Cook summed up. "Something that we've all dreamed of. Growing up watching Duke, watching Coach K win championships, celebrating with his great players. To be next to coach, he's been like a father to me over these last four years. To have his arm around me and hugging me while we're watching One Shining Moment was probably the best feeling in my life."

3. The 1998-99 team won 32 straight games. The streak ended in the NCAA title game, a close and bitter loss to Connecticut.

Had the final 30 seconds of that title game played out differently, then the 1999 Duke team would be considered the best team in Duke history, and one of the best teams in NCAA history.

If that sounds like hyperbole, consider these facts. Duke averaged 91.8 points per game, the second-best in school history (behind 1965), while allowing only 67.2. That's a point differential of 24.6, the best in ACC history.

Sophomore center Elton Brand and redshirt senior shooting guard Trajan Langdon were voted first-team All-ACC. Sophomore point guard William Avery was voted second-team

All-ACC. Junior forward Chris Carrawell and sophomore forward Shane Battier were voted third-team All-ACC.

This remains the only team in ACC history to have five all-conference players.

Freshman sixth man Corey Maggette could only garner 18 minutes per game. He went to the pros after the season and played 14 seasons in the NBA.

Brand was the first pick in the 1999 NBA draft and was joined by Maggette, Avery, and Langdon.

Brand was the ACC and National Player of the Year. Carrawell and Battier would follow him as ACC Player of the Year the next two seasons. No other ACC team has ever had three different players win this award in three consecutive seasons. Battier would be consensus National Player of the Year in 2001. Brand and Battier remain the only players from the same school and class to be consensus National Player of the Year.

Duke went 16-0 in the ACC and won the conference tournament. No one else has ever gone 19-0 in the ACC.

Duke was coming off a 32-4 season and began the season ranked at the top of the AP poll. That 1998 season might have been even better had Brand not missed 15 games with a broken foot.

Elton Brand slams one home. (AP Photo/Dave Martin)

Duke played in the Great Alaska Shootout, a homecoming for Langdon, an Anchorage native. Duke lost to Cincinnati, 77-75.

Duke shook it off, beating ninth-ranked Michigan State in a neutral-site contest and putting together blowout victories over NC State, Florida, and Michigan.

Duke actually led Michigan 34-2 at one point of their match.

By this point it was obvious that Brand was one of the nation's best players. Krzyzewski had to light his fire one time, bringing him off the bench after a lackluster game against Florida.

He didn't have to do it a second time.

Brand was a 6-foot-8, 260-pounder from Peekskill, New York. He was effective in the ways one would expect from a great player that size. Brand was a dominant rebounder and back-to-the-basket scorer. But he could finish a fast break, hit a 15-foot face up jumper, and protect the rim; he averaged over two blocks per game that season.

Brand had 22 points against Kentucky, 33 points against Virginia, and 27 points and 13 rebounds against Florida State, all double-digit wins.

In fact, they were almost all double-digit wins that season. Brand's close-to-the-basket skills and Langdon's downtown bombs made Duke difficult to guard in a half-court game, but this team really loved to run.

Duke beat ACC teams by scores like 99-58, 115-69, 100-54, and 102-71. Duke beat Florida 116-86. Nationally-ranked North Carolina fell by 12 and 20.

Duke's dominance of the ACC can best be seen by what they did to a talented Maryland team. Led by Steve Francis, the Terps were ranked fourth in the national poll when they hosted

Duke on January 3. It was tied at the half, but Duke used a 13-0 run right after intermission and pulled away to an 82-64 win. Duke handled Maryland 95-77 at Cameron later that season.

There were some challenges. Duke sleepwalked through the first half at Georgia Tech but flipped the switch and turned a 51-41 Tech lead early in the second half into an 87-79 Duke win.

The toughest test came in fabled Madison Square Garden, against eighth-ranked St. John's. Duke had several double-digit leads but couldn't hold any of them. St. John's hounded Avery into an uncharacteristic seven turnovers. Avery, Brand, and Duke backup Nate James fouled out, as did four St. John's players.

Ron Artest hit a 3 with a second left to send the game to overtime, at 81-81.

Duke fell behind by three in overtime, but Battier put Duke up 85-84 with a follow shot and Carrawell sewed it up from the line.

Taking over at point guard when Avery fouled out, Carrawell finished with 17 points, nine rebounds, and six assists.

St. John's forward Marvis "Bootsy" Thornton scored 40 points.

The 92-88 win would be Duke's closest victory of the season.

Duke shook off a Langdon sprained ankle and blitzed the ACC Tournament field, winning by 37, 15, and 23.

It wasn't any tougher in the East Regional, with victories of 99-58, 97-56, 78-61, and then 85-64 over Temple in the Elite Eight.

Duke went to the Final Four 36-1, riding a 31-game winning streak and seemingly invincible.

Duke had regained the top spot in the AP poll. But second-ranked Michigan State and third-ranked Connecticut lay in waiting.

Duke opened with Michigan State, a rematch. Many of these MSU players would help them win the 2000 NCAA title.

Brand dominated, with 18 points, 15 rebounds, and a block.

Duke led 32-20 at the half and nursed a double-digit lead most of the second half, winning 68-62.

Connecticut defeated Ohio State in the other semifinal.

Duke was an eight-point favorite against UConn, but didn't play like it.

Lots of explanations have been offered for Duke's performance that night in St. Petersburg. The ACC was down in 1999. Four of Duke's top six players were sophomores or freshmen, and their youth showed up. The Michigan State game took too much out of Duke.

All of which was probably true. But Connecticut only lost twice that season—against Syracuse and Miami—and UConn actually spent more time ranked No. 1 than Duke.

Avery struggled, missing nine of his 12 shots. Connecticut doubled Brand every time he touched the ball. Brand fought through it for 15 points and 13 rebounds, but he wasn't dominant. Carrawell and Battier shot five for 14, Duke didn't get a single second-half point from its bench, and the best rebounding team of Mike Krzyzewski's Duke tenure lost the battle of the boards 38-27. Duke couldn't handle Connecticut All-America player Richard Hamilton, who led everyone with 27 points.

Duke still was in it at the end. Langdon kept Duke in it, hitting five 3-pointers, the last making it 73-72 Connecticut. The Huskies scored and Avery answered with two foul shots.

Duke got a stop with just under a half minute left and a chance to win it all.

Brand had been Duke's go-to guy all season. But UConn had been smothering him all night.

"I give those guys credit," Brand said following the game. "They were fighting for position every time I touched it."

Langdon had the hot hand, 25 points worth. Duke called his number. He drove on Ricky Moore, there was contact, and a whistle.

Foul? Or something else? Langdon shot 86 percent from the line for his career.

Duke wanted him on the line.

They didn't get it. He was called for traveling. Duke fouled and Khalid El-Amin extended the lead to three from the line, with 5.2 seconds left.

Krzyzewski elected to not call timeout. "That's the way we play," he said after the game. "I think it's aggressive and it's winning and you know we're going for the win."

Langdon never got off a shot, losing the ball in traffic, his second turnover in 20 seconds, his only turnovers of the game.

It ended 77-74.

Years later, Langdon reflected.

"I still think we were the better team but that night they played more focused than us. I could sense there was something missing. But it was a one-possession game and could have gone either way. It was an incredible experience."

4. Duke won five straight, from 1999 through 2003. The margins of victory in the title games were 23, 13, 26, 30, and seven points.

Duke has had better NCAA Tournament runs and better regular-season runs. But no one has ever dominated the

ACC Tournament the way Duke did in this stretch, with 15 consecutive wins by an average margin of 17 points per game. Only four of these victories were by single digits, the closest an 84-82 win over Maryland in the 2001 semifinals.

Duke had to overcome a second-half, double-digit deficit to defeat the Terps in this game and had to do so again to beat NC State 84-77 in the 2003 title game.

Each one of these five Duke teams had at least one of Elton Brand, Shane Battier, Jason Williams, or J.J Redick, all of whom would be a consensus National Player of the Year at Duke.

But Nate James won that Maryland game with a last-second tip-in, while Daniel Ewing captured the Outstanding Player award in 2003 after scoring 62 points in three games.

The streak didn't end easily. Duke made it back to the finals in 2004 against Maryland and led most of the second half. Duke couldn't hold a late lead and fell in overtime, losing 95-87 and ending a 17-game winning streak in college basketball's most prestigious conference tournament.

Duke came back and won it again in 2005 and 2006. Redick was elected the Outstanding Player both times. He remains the only Duke player so honored.

This means that over an eight-year period, Duke went 23-1 in the ACC Tournament, the only loss in overtime, and just one regulation point away from winning eight straight championships.

Three other ACC teams have won three straight. NC State captured the first three ACC Tournaments, 1954–1956. North Carolina won it all from 1967 to 1969. Duke won it in 2009, 2010, and 2011.

5. Duke went 37-3 in 1986, setting a single-season record for wins that would be equaled but not bettered until Kentucky won 38 games in 2012. Starting four seniors, Duke went all the way to the NCAA championship game, losing to Louisville in the final seconds.

The 1986 season was the culmination of a four-year rebuilding project. Mike Krzyzewski started four freshmen the 1983 season, losing 17 games in the process.

But Duke got better, winning 24 games in 1984 and taking Krzyzewski to his first NCAA Tournament. The Blue Devils started the 1985 season 12-0, rising to second in the AP poll.

Duke couldn't sustain that, losing to Maryland and Wake Forest by two points. Duke defeated sixth-ranked North Carolina on the road, ending a 19-year losing streak in Chapel Hill. Duke had a chance for a share of the ACC regular-season title but lost at home to the Tar Heels and finished the ACC at 8-6.

Then the injury bug hit. Mark Alarie suffered a hip pointer in the ACC Tournament and David Henderson sprained an ankle in the NCAA Tournament, a 74-73 loss that ended Duke's season at 23-8.

Four key seniors returned for 1986. Johnny Dawkins was the nation's top guard, a slashing, athletic, 6-foot-2 scorer. He would win the 1986 Naismith Award, as the nation's top player.

Alarie was another All-American, a 6-foot-8, 220-pound forward, a superb defender, the team's best rebounder, and Krzyzewski's first "stretch four," a power forward big enough and strong enough to do the dirty work inside but sufficiently skilled offensively to stretch opposing defenses.

The 6-foot-5 Henderson was a tough wing, perhaps Duke's best clutch scorer. Jay Bilas was a natural forward at 6-foot-8 but played center.

Tommy Amaker was the fifth key returnee. Amaker was a junior and a classic point guard.

Dawkins had played point guard as a freshman in 1983 and had played it well, averaging 18 points and five assists per game. But he was more effective playing off the ball, and Amaker's arrival gave him that chance.

"Tommy gave me the freedom to make plays," he explained. "I wanted to attack, to beat the other team down the court, and he gave me that opportunity."

This team was so talented that 6-foot-10 Danny Ferry, the nation's top high school player in 1985, was a willing role player.

There was an early complication. Bilas had off-season knee surgery and sat out the first six games. Krzyzewski brought him along slowly, starting Ferry until midseason.

Krzyzewski put together a challenging schedule. Without Bilas, Duke defeated 18th-ranked St. John's 71-70 and fifth-ranked Kansas 92-86 to win the Big Apple NIT, at Madison Square Garden. Dawkins hit the game-winner against St. John's, while Henderson had a career-high 30 points against Kansas.

Duke started 16-0 and moved up to No. 2 in the AP poll, behind North Carolina. Duke went eight miles down the road on January 18 to play in the first game at the Dean E. Smith Center, aka the Dean Dome, and lost a classic, 95-92.

Three days later Duke fell at fourth-ranked Georgia Tech 87-80.

Duke wouldn't lose again for 10 weeks.

The most impressive weekend came in mid-February. On Saturday night, February 15, Duke went to Raleigh and defeated 17th-ranked NC State 72-70. The following afternoon

Duke edged 14th-ranked Notre Dame 75-74. Dawkins beat State with two foul shots with a second left and blocked a David Rivers shot at the buzzer to defeat the Irish.

Duke avenged the road losses to North Carolina and Georgia Tech and jumped to number one after defeating 10th-ranked Oklahoma, one of 11 victories Duke would post that season over ranked teams.

Duke clinched the ACC regular-season title with an 82-74 victory over North Carolina.

The ACC Tournament opened with Duke, North Carolina, and Georgia Tech ranked first, fourth, and sixth nationally.

Duke cruised to a 68-60 win over Wake Forest and had to work for a 75-70 win over Virginia.

On the other side of the bracket, Maryland stunned North Carolina in the opener and then fell to Georgia Tech.

The title game matched Duke's seniors against Tech seniors Mark Price and John Salley, who would go on to play 26 combined seasons in the NBA.

The result was one of the best ACC Tournament championship games ever, which featured two heavyweights going toe-to-toe for 40 minutes. The biggest margin was nine early in the game.

Duke led 37-34 at the half but trailed by a point when Alarie hit a jumper over Salley with seconds left. Tech missed, Dawkins made two foul shots, and Tech scored a meaningless basket, making the final 68-67.

Dawkins led everyone with 20 points and was named the tournament's outstanding player.

Duke opened the NCAAs in Greensboro five days later, matched against Mississippi Valley State, the winner of the SWAC Tournament.

It appeared to be an obvious mismatch.

Until it wasn't.

The game started at noon on a Thursday in a mostly empty Greensboro Coliseum. MVSU played with abandon and confidence while Duke played as if they had missed their wake-up call.

Duke trailed for 30 minutes.

Dawkins kept Duke afloat and provided the key points when Duke finally pulled away for the 85-78 win. He led everyone with 27 points, while Alarie finished strong for 19 points.

Duke demolished Old Dominion in the next game, 89-61, using an aggressive defense to hound ODU into 22 turnovers and 41 percent shooting.

Dawkins again led everyone, with 25 points.

Duke traveled north, to New Jersey and the Meadowlands. DePaul made them work in the Sweet Sixteen but fell 74-67. David Robinson and Navy were never competitive, and Duke won 71-50.

Dawkins was the leading scorer in both games, with 25 points against DePaul and 28 against Navy.

The 1986 Final Four was held in Dallas.

The top-ranked Blue Devils and second-ranked Kansas squared off in one semifinal, while seventh-ranked Louisville and unranked LSU met in the other.

Louisville fell behind early but dominated the second half in a low-drama 88-77 win.

Duke, on the other hand, had to overcome a tough and physical Kansas team.

Kansas led 65-61 with four minutes left. But the Blue Devils held Kansas to two points over those final minutes. Alarie tied the game at 65 with a dunk and Ferry put Duke up 69-67 with an offensive rebound.

Ferry drew a charge and Amaker finished the 71-67 scoring with two foul shots.

Dawkins scored 24 points. But Alarie was the unsung hero, holding Kansas star Danny Manning to 2-of-9 shooting from the field.

"It was a blood-on-the-floor kind of game," Alarie said. "We were exhausted, but somehow we had to suppress the fatigue and fight through it."

It was Duke's 37th win, breaking the old record of 36 set by Montana State in 1928 and equaled by them the following season and by Kentucky in 1948.

Duke and Louisville were opposites. Dawkins and Amaker gave the Blue Devils a big edge in perimeter quickness. But Louisville's leapers gave them an edge inside.

Each team exploited its advantages. Duke forced 24 Louisville turnovers and converted many of those into fast-break baskets. Louisville responded with a 38-23 advantage on the boards, second-chance points abounding.

Nevertheless, Duke led most of the game, and 37-34 at the half. A seven-point lead was the biggest margin the second half.

The Cardinals couldn't handle Dawkins early. He scored 13 of Duke's first 25 points and had 22 points with 15 minutes left when Louisville began double-teaming Dawkins every time he touched the ball.

This left his teammates with open shots. But Duke was playing its 40th game of the season and its second tough game in two days. The team was running on fumes.

"I was a shooter," Alarie said, "and shooters know. I kept taking shots that I knew were good, and they kept coming up short. It began to play on my mind."

Henderson agreed. "I didn't have any explosion. I was a half-step late for loose balls I usually chased down, rebounds I usually grabbed."

The key sequence came with 48 seconds left, when Louisville was coming off a timeout. There were still 11 seconds left on the shot clock (the NCAA had a 45-second shot clock but no 3-point shot in 1986).

Louisville ran some clock and Jeff Hall launched a long jumper. Air ball. Louisville's freshman center Pervis Ellison was having the best game of his career and he grabbed the rebound and laid it in a fraction before the shot clock expired.

Ellison ended the game with 25 points and 11 rebounds.

Duke still had a half-minute. But Henderson missed and Louisville closed it out from the line, 72-69 the final.

"It never occurred to us that we would lose," Alarie said. "Never."

The five seniors—reserve Weldon Williams was the fifth— scored 7,450 points at Duke; classmate Bill Jackman added 87 more in a single season before transferring. Dawkins (2,556) and Alarie (2,136) were the first players from the same class at the same school to score at least 2,000 points.

The season ended at 37-3.

Krzyzewski holds a special fondness for this transformative class and team.

"They defined the program. They became the example we've held up to every team since then, not just in how they played the game but in how they interacted with fans, how they handled classwork. They laid the foundation."

6. Duke lost to UCLA, 98-83 in 1964, the first title-game appearance for both programs.

Duke returned seven of its top nine players from its 1963 team, the first to make the Final Four.

But the losses included 1963 National Player of the Year Art Heyman.

Leading the incumbents was Jeff Mullins, a 6-foot-4 senior forward, who had averaged over 20 points and nine rebounds per game his first two seasons.

Mullins was joined in the starting lineup by classmates Jay Buckley and Buzzy Harrison and juniors Hack Tison and Denny Ferguson. Buckley and Tison were both around 6-foot-10, giants for that era.

Sophomores Jack Marin and Steve Vacendak led a productive bench.

Mullins was the undisputed star. Bubas had recruited him from Lexington, Kentucky. But Mullins actually grew up in Astoria, New York. His father worked for IBM and the family moved to Lexington when Jeff was in high school.

"I liked Bubas right away," Mullins said. "You could make two visits in those days. I visited in the fall and it was a cold, drizzly, dreary day. Fortunately, I came back in the spring, this time with my parents. It was a beautiful spring weekend, everything in bloom."

Mullins and Duke had some tough early tests. After beginning the season ranked fourth nationally, Duke moved up a spot after defeating seventh-ranked Ohio State and West Virginia to capture the West Virginia Centennial Tournament.

Mullins had 60 points in the two games.

But Duke fell at Vanderbilt (in overtime) and Michigan, the latter an 83-67 loss in which the thin Buckley and even thinner Tison were bludgeoned by a Michigan team that looked like it lived in a weight room.

The Wolverines out-rebounded Duke 61-35.

Another loss followed, 81-79 to Kentucky in the finals of the Sugar Bowl Tournament, in New Orleans, on New Year's Eve.

That dropped Duke to 7-3 and ninth in the AP poll.

The Blue Devils wouldn't lose again for seven weeks, tallying 10 wins in a row, including an 82-75 win over fourth-ranked Davidson.

Mullins had 29 points against Davidson.

Duke lost to Wake Forest 72-71 but finished the ACC with a 13-1 mark, 27-1 over consecutive years.

Duke cruised in the ACC Tournament, winning by 31, 16, and 21 points.

"That team knew how to win," Mullins said. "We really knew how to play together."

The NCAAs weren't seeded in those days. Third-ranked Duke got a first-round bye, while Villanova defeated Providence and set up a semifinal match between the two best teams in the East Regional. Ranked seventh in the AP poll, Villanova started four future pros.

Mullins met the challenge with one of the best individual performances in Duke history.

Villanova played a zone and Mullins kept finding holes in it. He had 26 points with seconds left in the first half when he hit a mid-court bomb to send Duke to the locker room with a 49-33 lead.

Duke maintained the margin after intermission and ended up with an 87-73 victory.

Mullins finished with 43 points, hitting 19 of 28 from the field.

It remains Duke's NCAA Tournament individual single-game scoring record.

Mullins also grabbed a dozen rebounds and held Richie Moore, Villanova's leading scorer, to eight points.

Connecticut upset Bill Bradley and Princeton in the other semifinal. But the Huskies were never competitive in the title game, still the worst Elite Eight beat-down in NCAA Tournament history. Mullins scored 30 points, as Duke won 101-54.

Duke was joined by Michigan, Kansas State, and an undefeated UCLA.

The semifinal match against Michigan gave Duke a chance to avenge the loss at Ann Arbor earlier in the season.

Buckley and Tison rose to the occasion, wrapping themselves around the Michigan big men and never letting them get away. The two big men combined for 37 points and 27 rebounds and Duke led Michigan on the boards by one rebound, 46-45.

Michigan's All-America wing Cazzie Russell kept the Wolverines in the game with 31 points. But Mullins countered with 21, all five Duke starters scored in double figures, and Duke led the entire second half, winning 91-80.

UCLA rallied late to edge Kansas State in the other semifinal.

The Final Four was played on a Friday/Saturday schedule in those days, leaving little time for the winners to recover.

The Bruins weren't very big—their tallest starter was 6-foot-5—and they had struggled in all of their wins leading up to the title game. Duke was a slight favorite.

They played the part of the favorite early, leading 30-27, with just under eight minutes left in the half.

Then it all fell apart. UCLA's trademark was a ferocious, full-court zone press, designed to not only stop opponents from scoring but also to generate easy, fast-break baskets.

The press clicked in a championship-deciding stretch of about three minutes when UCLA went on a 15-0 run by swarming over and then demoralizing Duke, turnover followed by layup, one after another.

It was 50-38 UCLA at the half, and Duke never got much closer in the second half.

The final was 98-83.

Mullins ended his college career with a solid 22-point performance.

"We put a lot of our eggs in the Michigan basket," Mullins said, years later. "An extra day off might have helped. But UCLA was so good. Who knows?"

Duke finished 26-5 and wouldn't make it back to the title game for 14 years.

Mullins had more games to play. He made the 1964 (Tokyo) U.S. Olympic Men's Basketball Team, Duke's first hoops Olympian. Mullins scored 18 points as the U.S. won the gold medal.

Mullins went on to lead a highly successful 12-year NBA career, scoring over 13,000 points and playing in three All-Star games.

7. NC State defeated Duke 12-10 in the 1968 ACC Tournament. There was no shot clock in those days and the loss knocked out Duke's NCAA hopes.

Duke entered the tournament seeded second, with an 11-3 conference mark. NC State was the third seed, at 9-5. Duke was ranked sixth in the AP poll, while NC State was unranked.

Mike Lewis, a 6-foot-8, 230-pound All-America center, led the 1968 Duke team. Lewis dominated in two regular-season wins over State.

Duke was big but not especially quick. And the Blue Devils played lots of zone.

NC State was quicker than Duke but smaller. Holding the ball made sense and State coach Norm Sloan was no dummy.

But why would Bubas order his team to stay back in its zone?

Bubas has always maintained that Duke would not have been able to chase down the quicker team. His team's best chance to win was to bide its time.

Duke had faced the same dilemma two years earlier, this time against North Carolina. Duke prevailed, 21-20, keeping alive a season that ended in the Final Four.

It didn't take long for the game to settle into something halfway between tedium and farce. The Wolfpack held the ball for a long eight minutes in the first half, lazily playing catch near midcourt, while Duke stayed back in a zone.

Sporadic deviations from this pattern resulted in a 4-2 Duke lead at intermission.

The spread disappeared for a few minutes early in the second half. Duke led 8-6, with 16:15 left, when Sloan again made the decision to pull the ball back out.

State's Bill Kretzer received a pass and held the ball near midcourt for much of the half.

State's Eddie Biedenbach went over to the sideline to consult with Sloan. Duke's Tony Barone followed him, only to be angrily shooed away by Sloan. Bored fans started throwing pennies on the floor. Referee Otis Almond picked them up and jokingly complained after the game that no one threw quarters.

State started looking for a shot with about three minutes left. Biedenbach hit a jumper, tying the game at 8.

The clock read 2:29.

Duke probed until Dave Golden was fouled in the act of shooting, with 43 seconds left.

Golden made the first foul shot but missed the second. Lewis grabbed the rebound but was called for traveling.

State got the ball to Kretzer, who was fouled. He tied the game with the first foul shot but also missed the second. His teammate Dick Braucher grabbed the rebound and scored inside.

Duke was down 10-9. Golden double-dribbled with 22 seconds left.

Duke fouled Van Williford, who made his only foul shot.

Trailing 11-9, Duke again got the ball to Golden, who again drew the foul. He made the first shot but missed the second, and Duke lost the rebound out of bounds.

Braucher was fouled and made the foul shot. Duke turned it over as the clock hit zero.

Duke ended the game shooting 2-11 from the field.

Sloan had no apologies.

"We felt like they would have to come out and play us. We have no reservations about playing that way. We played to win."

The Wolfpack advanced to the title game, where top-seeded North Carolina mauled them 87-50, still the most one-sided ACC Tournament title game ever.

Records are made to be broken, or so the cliché goes. But with the advent of shot clocks, this 12-10 record-low final score figures to last about as long as a record can last.

8. Randy Denton. A 6-foot-11 center, Denton averaged 12.7 rebounds per game from 1969 through 1971. Playing one year for Vic Bubas and two for Bucky Waters, Denton led Duke in scoring and rebounding all three of his varsity seasons.

Denton was one of the rare North Carolinians recruited by Bubas and was the only Duke player from North Carolina to make All-ACC between Carroll Youngkin (Winston-Salem) in 1959 and Jeff Capel (Fayetteville) in 1996.

Denton overwhelmed opponents close to the basket. In three seasons at Duke, he averaged 19.7 points per game, sixth in Duke history. He has three of the five best rebounding seasons (by average) in Duke history and nine of the 29 best single-game rebounding efforts, including a 25-rebound effort against Northwestern during his senior year that is second in school history. He, Art Heyman, and Danny Ferry are the only players to lead Duke in scoring and rebounding in three seasons.

Ironically, Denton never led the ACC in rebounding, finishing second three times to South Carolina's Tom Owens. Owens averaged 12.86 rebounds per game in 1971, Denton 12.83.

Duke was 52-32 during Denton's career and played in the NIT in 1970 and 1971. But Denton never played in an NCAA Tournament game and Duke lost its ACC Tournament opener in both his junior and senior seasons.

He also didn't have a lot of help. Denton was second-team All-ACC in 1969 and 1970 and first-team in 1971. But he was the only Blue Devil in that three-year span to make any All-ACC team.

Denton had some of his best games against elite competition. He grabbed 23 rebounds against fifth-ranked Davidson in 1969, 27 points against Rudy Tomjanovich and Michigan the following season, 28 points and 21 rebounds against Dan Issel and Kentucky in the Kentucky Invitational, 35 points and 16 rebounds against Michigan as a senior, and 35 points in a 1970 NIT loss.

"For some reason I was always focused against the top big men," Denton recalled. "I didn't want to embarrass myself."

His career high was 37 points at Clemson in 1970.

Randy Denton (31) focuses on blocking the shot against Tennessee in a 1971 NIT game. (AP Photo/JJL)

Denton ended his Duke career in the 1971 NIT, scoring 73 points, with 57 rebounds in four games as Duke finished in fourth place. Denton's 32 points and 18 rebounds keyed a quarterfinal win over Tennessee.

9. The 1965-66 team reached that spot midway in a promising season that ended in the Final Four. Absent stray bacteria, Duke might well have cut down the nets.

Duke returned four of its top six players from a 20-5 1965 team, including the top three scorers—guards Bob Verga and Steve Vacendak and forward Jack Marin.

Sixth man Bob Riedy moved into the starting lineup, while 6-foot-8, 230-pound sophomore Mike Lewis took over for graduated Hack Tison at center.

The 6-foot-6 Marin was the ACC's most versatile player; in fact, Bubas has long maintained that Marin was the most versatile player he ever coached. Verga was the ACC's best perimeter shooter, Lewis the best rebounder, and Vacendak the top playmaker.

Bubas didn't go too deep into his bench. But everybody played their natural position, Bubas started two seniors (Marin and Vacendak) and two juniors (Verga and Riedy), and his team could shoot, handle, defend, and rebound. Duke outrebounded opponents by 12.7 rebounds per game, the best differential in school history.

Duke began the season ranked third in the AP poll, behind two-time defending national champion UCLA and Michigan.

The Blue Devils opened with wins over Virginia Tech and Clemson but fell at South Carolina 73-71 and dropped to sixth.

Next up would be UCLA, in a pair of games. The Bruins were still undefeated and atop the polls.

Duke won both games convincingly, 82-66 and 94-75. Marin led Duke in both games, with 20 and 23 points, respectively.

It turned out that this was not one of John Wooden's great UCLA teams. They ended the season 18-8.

But nobody knew that at the time, and Duke leapfrogged everyone to take the top spot in both the AP and UPI polls.

Duke solidified that hold 10 days later when they edged third-ranked Michigan 100-93, in an overtime contest held in

Detroit. Marin and Michigan's Cazzie Russell—who would win the National Player of the Year award for the season—matched each other with 30 points, with Verga adding 27.

Duke shot 52.6 percent from the field and overcame an eight-point halftime deficit to win in a hostile environment over a team that would advance to the Elite Eight, a win more impressive in retrospect than either UCLA win.

The Blue Devils won 13 straight after the South Carolina loss and held on to the top spot in the AP poll for eight weeks.

It ended on the night of February 7 in Charleston, West Virginia, where Duke fell to West Virginia 94-90.

Duke fell to second in the polls and wouldn't be ranked number one again until the beginning of the 1978-79 season, three coaches later.

One of those Duke coaches would be Bucky Waters, who coached West Virginia to that 1966 upset.

Duke continued to dominate the ACC, a stunning loss at Wake Forest notwithstanding. Duke ended the ACC schedule with a 12-2 record, three games ahead of second-place NC State.

Duke was ranked second nationally, trailing only Kentucky but needing to win the conference tournament to keep its season alive.

The Blue Devils avenged the Wake Forest loss in the opener, 103-73, behind Verga's 29 points.

Duke crushed Wake Forest on the boards, 57-26, with Riedy grabbing 14.

North Carolina was next. Duke had defeated the Tar Heels twice in the regular season, 88-77 and 77-63.

Having run with Duke twice and having nothing to show for it, North Carolina coach Dean Smith tried another tactic—his four corners—a stalling tactic designed to pull Duke out of its 2-3 zone and turn them into chasers.

The result was 40 minutes of cat and mouse. Vacendak—Duke's best defender—picked up three early fouls and Bubas elected to play it close to the vest.

The half ended at 7-5.

The action picked up after intermission. North Carolina's Bob Lewis converted a three-point play to put the Tar Heels up 12-8 and another to make it 17-12.

A Vacendak jumper made it 17-15, but Larry Miller scored on a follow shot and it was 19-15, with about five minutes remaining.

Two foul shots by Marin, a foul shot by Mike Lewis, and a jumper by Vacendak tied the game at 20.

It was decided at the foul line. North Carolina's John Yokley missed a freebie with 1:40 left.

Duke held for the final shot. Mike Lewis got loose and was fouled on a shot, with four seconds left. Lewis missed the first but made the second. UNC threw the ball away on the inbounds pass and Duke escaped with a 21-20 win.

Smith was unapologetic after the game. "I thought we deserved victory. We had tried to go up and down with them twice and lost."

Bubas didn't sound happy about UNC's approach. "I have no comment on their style of play. It's in the rulebook and a coach can elect to use it. That's his decision."

The Blue Devils could be forgiven if they had a bad sense of déjà vu after falling behind early by nine against NC State in the title game. One season earlier, top-seeded Duke had fallen in the championship contest to NC State.

Duke trailed by a point at intermission and took the lead for good at 64-63, when Vacendak scored with 3:43 left.

The final was 71-66. All five starters scored in double figures for Duke, which again dominated on the boards, 45-31.

The 1966 East Region had six teams. Duke got a bye in the opening round and met first-round winner St. Joseph's in the second round.

Bubas and Duke had bested Jack Ramsay and St. Joseph's in the 1960 and 1963 NCAA Tournaments and continued the trend in 1966.

But it wasn't easy. St. Joseph's went into the Duke game 23-4, ranked fifth nationally. Duke led most of the game but never by very much, squeaking by in the 76-74 victory. Verga and Marin led Duke with 22 and 18 points respectively.

Duke and Syracuse met in the regional final, the first meeting of these storied programs. Duke's zone flummoxed Syracuse star Dave Bing into a 4-14 shooting night and Duke won 91-81.

All five Duke starters scored in double figures, led by Marin (22), Verga (21), and Vacendak (19).

The 1966 Final Four was held at Cole Field House on the campus of the University of Maryland. The field was top-ranked Kentucky, second-ranked Duke, third-ranked Texas Western (now Texas–El Paso), and dark horse Utah.

Duke thought it had a great shot at Kentucky. The Wildcats didn't start anyone taller than 6-foot-5—they were known as Rupp's Runts—and Duke was a dominant team inside.

But a few days before the game, news leaked out that Verga was running a high fever, with fatigue and aches.

Verga was averaging 19 points per game, and Duke did not have much scoring available on the bench.

The illness has been called strep throat, influenza, bronchitis, or pneumonia. But a rose is a rose, and Verga was very sick.

Verga was ineffective, scoring four points, missing five of seven shots. He sat out most of the second half.

Marin kept Duke afloat, with 29 points and seven rebounds. Lewis added 21 points. But Rupp's Runts out-rebounded Duke 33-29 and the Blue Devils fell 83-79.

Duke defeated Utah 79-77 in the consolation game, as Bubas played 11 players. Verga's fever broke earlier in the day and he scored 15 points.

Texas Western defeated Kentucky in the now-famous title game, using only black players against Kentucky's all-white lineup.

Would Duke have defeated Kentucky with a healthy Verga?

An unanswerable question. But the consolation game was Bubas's last NCAA Tournament game and Duke's last appearance in the Big Dance until 1978, easily the longest gap since Duke's first appearance in 1955.

10. Danny Ferry scored 58 points against Miami on December 10, 1988, early in his senior season. This broke the school record of 48 set by Dick Groat in 1952. It also broke the ACC record of 57 points set by NC State's David Thompson in 1974, against Buffalo State.

Miami was not yet an ACC school when it hosted Duke, the Blue Devils' first trip to Miami in 26 years.

Miami was small but quick and thought an up-tempo game provided them the best chance of an upset.

What Miami couldn't do was handle Ferry.

Ferry scored inside, outside, from the line, and in transition. By the time Duke's 117-102 victory was over Ferry had connected on 23 of 26 from the field and 10 for 12

Danny Ferry scores two of his 58 points against Miami in December 1988. (AP Photo/Kathy Willens)

from the foul line. Only two of his successful field goals were 3-pointers.

"I was totally in a zone," he said later. "My mind was so clear and focused. See ball, catch ball, shoot ball."

11. 1960. Vic Bubas took his first Duke team to five postseason victories, finishing one game short of the Final Four.

Harold Bradley's last Duke team had gone a mediocre 13-12.

But that team was led by a core of sophomores, back in an era when sophomores were considered young.

Bubas inherited Carroll Youngkin, a strong 6-foot-6 center; Doug Kistler, a lanky 6-foot-9 shooter; Howard Hurt, a versatile 6-foot-3 wing; and John Frye, a 6-foot playmaker.

There were growing pains. Bubas lost his first game at Duke, 59-49 against Georgia Tech and lost twice in the Dixie Classic. Duke lost four straight ACC road games and finished the regular season at 7-7 in the ACC, good enough for fourth place.

The Blue Devils entered the ACC Tournament having lost five of its last seven.

Duke opened against fifth-place South Carolina. Bubas's squad controlled the game almost from the beginning, winning 82-69.

Duke was joined in the semifinals by Wake Forest, North Carolina, and NC State, the four North Carolina schools.

North Carolina and Wake Forest were the league's two powers that season, each 12-2 in the ACC.

Duke played North Carolina in one semifinal and there was little reason to see Duke as anything more than a speed-bump on the road to the inevitable North Carolina–Wake Forest title game. After all, led by ACC Player of the Year and future NBA All-Star Lee Shaffer, the Tar Heels had pounded Duke three times already, 75-53 in the Dixie Classic and 84-57 and 75-50 in the conference matches.

Bubas told the media that he had North Carolina right where he wanted them. "I like the psychological spot we're in. We've got all to win and nothing to lose."

Duke played a 1-3-1 zone that completely flummoxed the favorites. The Tar Heels went six minutes without a field goal and fell behind 35-19.

North Carolina closed to 35-23 at the half and continued to chip away at Duke's lead, taking a 50-49 lead on a Shaffer field goal with nine minutes left.

Duke held on for the 71-69 victory. Youngkin dominated inside, helping foul out both Shaffer and starting center Ray Stanley. He scored 30 points, hitting 12-19 from the field and 6-11 from the line, with 17 rebounds.

Wake Forest defeated North Carolina State 71-66 in the other semifinal, a game enlivened by a fight between Wake Forest's Dave Budd and NC State's Anton Muehlbacher.

ACC commissioner Jim Weaver suspended Budd from the title game.

Wake Forest head coach Bones McKinney psyched his team to a fever pitch, citing Budd's suspension as a great injustice.

Shortly before the game started, Wake received word that the ACC's executive committee had overruled Weaver and reinstated Budd.

McKinney later wrote that the decision took the steam out of his team.

Or perhaps Duke was just better that night. Wake had defeated Duke by 17 and 19 points earlier that season, but Duke was now more focused and motivated.

This time it was Kistler who dealt the heaviest blows, making 10 of 15 from the field.

Len Chappell matched Kistler for Wake, but the Demon Deacons struggled against Duke's zone.

A Kistler jumper gave Duke a 59-58 lead with 1:40 left. Duke got two big defensive stops and Frye locked up the 63-59 win with four foul shots.

Tournament MVP Kistler led everyone with 22 points, and also added nine rebounds.

Duke had three days to get ready for the opening round of the NCAA Tournament.

It was a curious setup. The East Regional had seven teams. St. Joseph's got a first-round bye, while the other six teams played a triple-header in New York's Madison Square Garden.

Duke drew Ivy League champion Princeton.

Bubas had tournament experience, both as a player and as an assistant coach. He focused his team and maximized Duke's huge size differential—Princeton's tallest starter was 6-foot-3—by pounding the ball inside.

Kistler had 26 points, Youngkin pulled down 16 rebounds, and Duke won the battle of the boards 45-29. Duke led 41-26 at the half and cruised to an 84-60 win, the first NCAA Tournament win in school history.

NYU defeated Connecticut and West Virginia defeated Navy in the other games.

A Jack Ramsay–led St. Joe's, one of the nation's top programs, was next.

Both teams' defenses were better than their opponents' offenses. Baskets were hard to come by. Led by Hurt's 13 first-half points, Duke got some separation late in the first half, taking a 27-20 lead at intermission.

Duke extended its lead to 38-27 at the midpoint of the second half before St. Joe's trademark press began to take a toll. Youngkin fouled out on a charge with 1:15 left and St. Joseph's cut the Duke lead to 56-54.

Duke had a chance to salt it away from the foul line. John Frye and then Bizz Mewhort each converted the first end of a one-and-one but each missed the second, leaving Duke with a 58-54 lead and seconds remaining.

Paul Westhead—later a well-known coach —scored inside to cut the Duke lead to two, with 20 seconds left.

Frye missed the first end of a one-and-one, and St. Joe's rushed the ball down court. They missed the shot, Duke knocked the ball out of bounds, and the clock continued to run, hitting zero before St. Joe's could inbounds the ball.

Duke turned it over 20 times but made enough shots to hold off the cold-shooting Hawks; St. Joseph's shot 29.7 percent from the field.

Youngkin led Duke with 22 points.

NYU upset Jerry West and West Virginia in the other semifinal.

The regional title game was close for about 10 minutes. At that point NYU went on a 12-2 run that extended a 16-13 lead to 28-15.

Trailing by double digits, Duke came out of its zone into a man-to-man. NYU's star center Tom "Satch" Sanders (he would go on to play 13 seasons for the Boston Celtics) exploited that defense. The Blue Devils—playing their sixth game in 10 days—never made a second-half run.

The final was 74-59. Kistler led Duke with 20 points, while Sanders had 22 points and 16 rebounds for the victors.

Duke had better teams in 1961 and 1962 but couldn't recapture the ACC Tournament magic. Yet Bubas broke through to the Final Four in 1963 and 1964. The foundation of those runs was laid in 1960.

12. Jim Spanarkel scored 2,012 points in a Duke career that lasted from 1976 through 1979. The 6-foot-5 guard averaged 17.6 points per game.

Jim Spanarkel was from Jersey City, New Jersey. He wasn't exactly a recruiting afterthought at Hudson Catholic High School, but his teammate Mike O'Koren, one year Spanarkel's junior, was the prepster who set hearts aflutter.

Spanarkel wasn't an elite run-jump athlete. Duke didn't keep official dunk statistics in those days, but if Spanarkel ever notched a dunk in a college game, you could count them on one hand.

However, Spanarkel more than made up for any athletic deficiencies. His basketball IQ was off the charts. He was almost always in the right place, doing the right thing. Spanarkel developed an excellent skill set, and he was both a fierce competitor and a quiet leader.

Spanarkel was also an outstanding baseball player, a right-handed pitcher who had picked Duke in part because Bill Foster assured him he would be allowed to play both basketball and baseball.

Spanarkel arrived at Duke at a time when the Blue Devils' fortunes were at a low point, a 10-16 mark when Spanarkel was a high school junior, 13-13 when he was a senior, which also was Foster's first season at Duke.

Duke had five recruited guards ahead of Spanarkel. But it didn't take him long to put all but junior Tate Armstrong on the bench.

Years later, Foster explained it. "We knew we had something special early in practices. No matter how we divided up the teams, the team that Jim was on always seemed to win. He just had a knack for doing the right thing."

Spanarkel scored 12 points in his first game, a 103-72 win over Johns Hopkins. He averaged 13.3 per game and was voted ACC Freshman of the Year.

But Duke couldn't stop elite teams, couldn't win close games, and ended 13-14, 3-9 in the ACC.

Duke started the 1977 season 11-3 but collapsed down the stretch after star senior Tate Armstrong broke his right wrist. Already Duke's top defensive player, Spanarkel absorbed additional ball-handling and scoring responsibilities.

Duke dropped to 14-13, but not because of Spanarkel.

He ended the season averaging 19.2 points, 5.4 rebounds, 3.5 assists, and 2.6 steals per game, while shooting 52 percent from the field and 84 percent from the line. All this he accomplished in almost 38 minutes per game.

He also took over as team leader, an unusual responsibility for a sophomore. Armstrong's injury "helped my advancement as a player, but it also gave me an opportunity to be a leader and take charge," he said later.

Spanarkel was named second-team All-ACC.

He also pitched for the Duke baseball team for the second and final season before committing fully to basketball.

Spanarkel's best season was 1978, Duke's magic-carpet-ride-season, which ended with Duke losing to Kentucky in the national title game.

Spanarkel was appointed captain before the beginning of the season.

No one complained. Kenny Dennard was a freshman that season, part of a significant talent upgrade. "I learned about leadership from Jim," Dennard said later. "You don't have to be a yeller or a loudmouth. You can lead by example if you have the respect and Jim had the respect. He didn't say much. So, if he had something to say, you knew it was important. You listened."

Spanarkel hit the national spotlight on January 4 in College Park, where he led Duke to an 88-78 win over Maryland, Duke's first win at Maryland since 1971. In fact, Maryland had won 10 of the previous 11 games between the two teams.

Spanarkel hit 12 of 20 from the field and 9 of 10 foul shots on the way to a 33-point game; he added five assists.

But it wasn't just the stat line that impressed *Washington Post* writer Ken Denlinger. He was just as impressed by Spanarkel's advanced understanding of angles and positions and situations, telling his readers that Maryland had been "Spanarkeled."

Duke lost its next game at NC State by 24 points and dropped two ACC games when Gminski injured a foot. Duke finished second in the ACC, one game behind North Carolina, with whom it split two conference games.

Then Spanarkel keyed a March run. Duke defeated Clemson, Maryland, and Wake Forest to win its first ACC Tournament title since 1966. Spanarkel scored 53 points and was voted the tournament's most valuable player.

The run continued, with wins over Rhode Island, the University of Pennsylvania, and Villanova putting Duke into the Final

Four, again Duke's first appearance since 1966. Spanarkel scored 61 points in those three games, shooting 23 for 38 from the field.

He continued the hot shooting, adding 41 total points in the Final Four (a win over Notre Dame) and a 94-88 loss to Kentucky in the title game. Spanarkel made all 12 of his foul shots against Notre Dame, helping hold off a late Irish rally.

Spanarkel's 1978 season was one of the best in Duke history. He led Duke in scoring (20.8), assists (3.7), and minutes played. His 86.3 percentage led the ACC in foul shooting, while his 93 steals still stands as a school record.

Jim Spanarkel splits a North Carolina double-team.
(AP Photo/Jordan)

Conventional wisdom suggests that 1979—Spanarkel's senior season—was a huge disappointment for the Blue Devils. And that's true to an extent. The 1978 title game ended with Duke fans chanting "we'll be back," a valid premise for a team that was starting one junior, two sophomores, and two freshmen.

And Spanarkel admits that some of the magic was gone in 1979. "There were additional pressures, more distractions, and more desire for individual recognition. The bar had been raised and we never clicked like we did in '78."

Nevertheless, Duke won the Big Four Tournament for

the first time in nine tries, started out 6-0, and never dropped out of the top 10. Duke and North Carolina shared the ACC regular-season title and Duke went into the postseason expecting a long run.

It all began to fall apart in the ACC Tournament. Duke defeated NC State 62-59 to advance to the title game against the Tar Heels. But starting point guard Bob Bender underwent an appendectomy following the victory over State and was lost for the season.

Duke subsequently fell to the Tar Heels, 71-63.

Then Dennard sprained an ankle, not in a game or a practice but messing around in a pickup game.

Duke played St. John's in the NCAA Tournament, 25 miles from home at Reynolds Coliseum, on the campus of North Carolina State University, minus two starters.

It got worse. Gminski had a stomach bug and was sick throughout the game.

Yet still Duke hung in there, Spanarkel trying to will his team to victory.

Spanarkel's last appearance in a Duke uniform was a typical one, in which he tallied 16 points, four rebounds, three assists, and two steals.

But it wasn't enough. Duke fell, 80-78.

Spanarkel ended the St. John's game with 2,012 points, the first Blue Devil to surpass the 2,000-point barrier. In fairness, players like Art Heyman, Jeff Mullins, and Bob Verga didn't have four years to attain that level. Spanarkel now ranks 11th in Duke career scoring, though his scoring average is 10th in school history. He ranks fourth in made free throws, ninth in free throw percentage (80.6), and first in steals per game.

More important than the stats is the fact that Spanarkel was a key player in the revival of Duke basketball at a time when many wondered if such a thing was even possible.

13. Chris Duhon amassed 301 steals in a four-year career that ended in the 2004 Final Four. Duhon also ranks second in minutes played and assists and third in assist to turnover ratio.

The lightning-quick Duhon came to Duke with a reputation as a scoring guard. He never scored much at Duke, but he did everything else. He averaged almost 30 minutes per game for Duke's 2001 national champions and that season was Mike Krzyzewski's first ACC Freshman of the Year.

Duhon led Duke in assists and steals in 2002, 2003, and 2004.

He was at his best as a senior. His career-best 10.0 points per game was fifth-best on the team. But his other contributions were so significant that he finished runner-up—to NC State's Julius Hodge—in voting for ACC Player of the Year and was voted third-team All-America by AP.

14. Chris Carrawell was a role player in 1999, a third-team All-ACC forward. He was an All-America player the following season.

This was a classic example of a player elevating his game to meet a need. Duke's loaded 1999 team didn't need scoring from Carrawell, a junior from St. Louis.

Then Trajan Langdon graduated and Elton Brand, William Avery, and Corey Maggette went to the NBA. Duke's top four scorers were now gone.

The 6-foot-6 Carrawell had always been a whatever-you-need kind of guy, guarding Wake Forest's Tim Duncan in a 1997 Duke win, or playing point guard against St. John's when Avery fouled out in 1999.

Carrawell was a good but not elite athlete and was an ordinary 3-point shooter. But he had an excellent mid-range game and an ability to find openings.

In 2000, he averaged 17 points per game and led Duke to a 15-1 ACC record and another ACC Tournament title, part of a four-year sequence in which Duke went 59-5 in the ACC.

Carrawell edged teammate Shane Battier for ACC Player of the Year.

Carrawell's take on his career? "It just goes to show that if you work hard, keep getting better, always stay hungry, then you have a chance to do some great things."

15. Dick Groat was named National Player of the Year in 1952, the year after he set a national scoring record with 831 points on the hardcourt and led the Duke baseball team to the College World Series. (As an aside, the national scoring record was total points scored and was partially the result of the fact that Duke played 33 games that year—an awful lot for a team that played in neither the NCAA or NIT tournaments.)

Dick Groat may be Duke's best two-sport athlete. He is most widely recognized for a 14-year career as a major league shortstop. His baseball career peaked in 1960, when he led the Pittsburgh Pirates to a World Series title over the heavily favored New York Yankees, led the National League with a .325 batting average that season, and was voted National League Most Valuable Player.

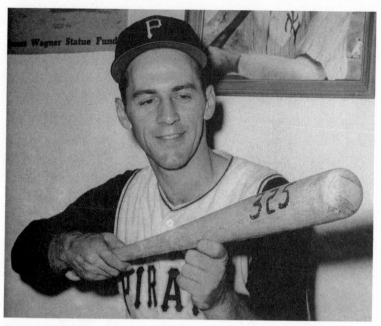

Former Duke baseball and basketball All-American Dick Groat shows off a bat from his 1960 MVP season for the Pittsburgh Pirates. (AP Photo)

Groat also started for the St. Louis Cardinals when they won the 1964 World Series, again in seven games against the Yankees.

Groat had 2,138 hits in the majors and was named to the National League All-Star team five times.

A baseball All-America athlete in 1951 and 1952, Groat batted .375 at Duke and led the Blue Devils to a third-place finish in the 1952 College World Series.

Groat came to Duke from the Pittsburgh suburb of Swissvale. At six feet tall, Groat was a good but not elite run-jump athlete. But he was smart, disciplined, skilled, and fiercely competitive.

Groat was alerted to Duke when his father ran across a laudatory article in *Sport* magazine on Jack Coombs and the Duke baseball program.

Groat has always maintained that basketball was his first love. But there's no doubt that he was a dual-sport athlete from the day he set foot on the Duke campus.

Groat only played a half-season of basketball in 1950, his sophomore season. Groat was academically ineligible for the second semester, after averaging 14.5 points per game for 19 games.

Groat took advantage of an unusual set of circumstances. Duke head coach Gerry Gerard had been diagnosed with terminal cancer and Duke had brought in 33-year-old Arnold "Red" Auerbach, who had just resigned as head coach of the NBA's Tri-Cities Blackhawks. Duke wanted Auerbach to take over for Gerard, but Auerbach left before Gerard stepped down.

Yet he did spend time helping Groat hone his game.

Groat later called Auerbach "the greatest teacher I've ever been associated with. We went one-on-one for months. He taught me lots of little tricks. It was hard work, but it gave me a huge advantage."

Groat also worked on his jump shot. The jump shot was less than a decade old in the early 1950s, and many of the game's best players still relied on the old-fashioned set shot. But Groat turned his into a formidable weapon.

Gerard's deteriorating health forced him to resign prior to the 1950-51 season.

He was replaced by Harold Bradley, whose fast-break offense was perfect for Groat, who emerged as one of the nation's best scorers. During a widely anticipated January 6, 1951 matchup with NC State's high-scoring guard, Sammy Ranzino, Groat went for 36 points.

Ranzino countered with 32 and State won 77-71 in overtime, by which point Groat had been sidelined with five fouls.

The 36 points was a school record that lasted all of three weeks, until he scored 37 against Davidson.

Groat scored 85 points in three games in the 1951 Southern Conference Tournament, 31 of those in the title game, a 67-63 loss to NC State.

A consensus second-team All-America player, Groat ended the season averaging 25.2 points per game, Duke's only double-figure scorer.

Groat was even better in 1952. Bradley integrated some talented sophomores, including rebounding star Bernie Janicki and guard Rudy D'Emilo, and the Blue Devils started 8-4, including two losses in the Dixie Classic.

Duke hit its stride, ending the regular season with a 13-game winning streak, including the team's first win over Everett Case's NC State in Raleigh.

Groat again broke his school record, with 46 points against George Washington.

He played his final home game against North Carolina, then in the midst of a rare downturn in their fortunes; Duke beat them eight straight times during this period, from February 1951 to February 1954.

Duke led the Tar Heels 50-32 at the half. But North Carolina closed to 56-48 and Duke began to go to its senior star on every possession.

It paid off, in a big way. Using his full arsenal—drives, jump shots, fast-break baskets, and free throws—Groat scored 31 points in the final 14 minutes.

The final was 94-64. Groat ended the game with 48 points, again breaking his school record. It's still the most points anyone has ever scored in Cameron Indoor Stadium.

Duke unofficially kept track of assists in 1952, and Groat was credited with 12. Groat accounted for 72 points that Saturday.

Duke went into the Southern Conference Tournament 22-5, ranked 12th in the AP poll.

Groat needed three wins to cap his college career with a bid to the NCAA Tournament.

Groat led Duke to a 51-48 win over Maryland, with 21 points, including the last three points of the game that broke a late 48-48 tie.

This contemporary account of that basket, as written in Raleigh's *News and Observer*, gives some idea of Groat's dynamism.

"He zoomed down court, weaved through four Terp defenders, and popped in two spectacular points."

Duke followed up that barn-burner with a 90-88 win over a 23-3 West Virginia team. Groat scored 31.

The West Virginia game was a tough, physical contest that left Duke ill-prepared for the title match against nemesis NC State.

Duke did lead early, 38-35 at the half. But the Blue Devils trailed 71-66 when Groat fouled out, and they ended up on the short end of a 77-68 score.

Groat scored 27, giving him 79 points in three tournament games and 164 in six elimination tournament games over two seasons; that's a 27.3 average.

Duke was invited to the NIT. But the school turned it down, concerned by the New York–centric point-shaving scandal just unfolding.

Duke ended its season 24-6, a school record for wins that would last until 1963.

Groat averaged 26 points per game, second in the nation to Kansas center Clyde Lovellette. It remains the third best single-season scoring average in Duke history.

And then he was off leading the Duke baseball team to Omaha.

UPI—the coaches poll—named Groat National Player of the Year, and both UPI and AP named him first-team All-America. Groat ended his Duke career with a 23.0 scoring average, still the second best in school history.

Duke retired Groat's number 12 jersey later that spring. He would be the only Duke player so honored until 1980.

16. Bill Foster. Foster coached at Bloomsburg State (D-2), Rutgers, and Utah before Duke and at South Carolina and Northwestern after Duke.

Foster's Duke tenure comprised only six of his 33 years as a head coach. Six other men coached longer at Duke.

Yet, that period was critical to Duke, reviving a moribund program, providing a bridge between Vic Bubas and the 1960s and the success of Foster's replacement at Duke, Mike Krzyzewski.

Foster grew up in Pennsylvania and attended Elizabethtown College in that state. Even while coaching in distant places, Foster returned to his home state every summer for clinics in the Pocono Mountains.

Foster coached in Philadelphia high schools before taking Bloomsburg State to a 45-11 mark in three seasons.

That led him to Rutgers, where he stayed for eight seasons, going 120-75 and taking the team to two NITs.

It would be his longest stay.

Rutgers would seem like the perfect place for Foster, a school with basketball resources, close to both his Pennsylvania roots and the fertile New York City recruiting area. His last Rutgers team went 16-7.

But Foster had a case of professional wanderlust. By his own admission he preferred building a program to sustaining a program. He needed to move along.

He moved almost to the other end of the country, the University of Utah.

Foster rebuilt Utah, taking the Utes to the 1974 NIT title game, where they lost to Purdue.

That was the same year Duke went 10-16, tallying the most losses in school history up to that point.

So, it makes sense that Duke would be looking for a new coach. But why would Foster look at Duke?

Duke was struggling in the mid-1970s. Bucky Waters's first two Duke teams went to the NIT but were led by players he had inherited from Vic Bubas. He couldn't replace that talent.

Waters's teams also suffered from attrition, as his drill-sergeant persona clashed with a different type of campus culture. Waters lost five ACC-level players to transfer in four seasons.

Duke went 14-12 in 1972 and 12-14 the following season, Duke's first losing season since 1939. Duke students started showing up with "Fire Bucky" signs, while season-ticket holders stayed home in droves.

Waters resigned days before practice began for the 1974 season, when athletic director Carl James declined to extend his expiring contract.

James approached Foster at that point. But Foster didn't want to leave Utah that close to the season. Neil McGeachy,

Waters's top assistant, ultimately took the job on short notice.

The ACC was a tough neighborhood in the mid-1970s. NC State won the 1974 NCAA title, Dean Smith was becoming an icon at North Carolina, and Maryland, Virginia, and Clemson were all at levels of program excellence.

For five years Foster even had to share his name with another Bill Foster, who coached at Clemson.

Like I said, tough neighborhood.

But Foster wanted a program to rebuild, and Duke needed rebuilding. Foster remembered Duke's 1960s greatness, and returning to the East Coast was a bonus.

Foster faced a talent deficit. For the only time ever, Duke didn't have an All-ACC player in 1974.

Foster made a conscious decision to play up-tempo basketball, both to appeal to a disgruntled fan base and more importantly to appeal to recruits.

The on-court results were sometimes dire. Duke scored 109 points against Wake Forest in 1975 and still lost by 13 points. NC State defeated Duke 106-101 and 96-95 in 1976. Duke averaged over 88 points per game in 1976 and still had a losing season because they couldn't defend good teams at that tempo.

But the fans responded and recruits noticed. In three consecutive classes, Foster brought in Jim Spanarkel, Mike Gminski, and Gene Banks, all of whom became All-America players.

Foster, subsequently, left for South Carolina after the Gamecocks' Frank McGuire announced that he was retiring after the 1980 season. In his six seasons at Duke, Foster had led the team to 113 victories—40 wins in his first three seasons there and 73 in the final three.

Foster had a distinct personality, characterized by wry, self-deprecating humor. But you don't win almost 500 games in college basketball without a strong competitive drive.

Foster was let go after a 12-16 record in 1986.

He didn't stay unemployed long. Northwestern was his last stop. Superficially, Northwestern and Duke were similar. Both are academically-oriented private schools, in power conferences dominated by larger, state-supported schools.

But Northwestern had no basketball tradition and Foster did nothing to change that, going 54-141 in seven seasons, only 13 of those wins coming in Big Ten play.

Despite the struggles at Northwestern, Foster's time at Duke tends to stand out as a bright spot in his college coaching career and helped pave the way for greater Duke basketball successes down the road.

17. Duke's Grayson Allen averaged 4.4 points per game as a freshman in 2015. He averaged 21.6 the following season, an increase of 17.2 points per game. Clemson's Will Solomon held the old record, improving from 6.3 points per game in 1999 to 20.9 in 2000, an increase of 14.6 points per game. Tate Armstrong held the old Duke record, going from 9.7 in 1976 to 24.2 in 1977 (increase of 14.5 PPG).

Allen led Duke with 3.5 assists per game.

Allen came to Duke in the same freshman class as Jahlil Okafor, Tyus Jones, and Justise Winslow. His classmates started the entire 2015 season and all three were selected in the first round of that year's NBA draft.

The 6-foot-5 Allen played little but erupted in the Final Four, scoring 25 points.

The graduation of Quinn Cook and the loss of the three freshmen to the draft provided an opening for Allen during the 2016 season, and he crashed through the door.

Early in the season Allen recognized both the opportunity and the responsibility.

"Last year I started to drive the ball well but when I drove, I had tunnel vision going to the basket and missing open guys. This year, I need to see the whole floor and find open guys."

Krzyzewski agreed.

"He's a unique player. He can defend, rebound. He can shoot. He can drive. He can play through a foul."

Allen started well but had a miserable game against Kentucky, scoring six points on 2-11 shooting, in a Duke loss.

The response speaks volumes about the way Duke approaches performance issues.

"I didn't make any adjustments in that game," Allen said. "I was very repetitive in my moves. It was a rough film session. He [Mike Krzyzewski] was just brutally honest with me. That's how he is as a coach and that's the way I want it. I just needed to make those adjustments, read the defense better."

Allen scored 30 points in his next game, against Virginia Commonwealth, and then 32 against Georgetown, the latter a stunningly efficient performance that included connecting on 9-12 from the field (5-6 on 3s) and 9-9 from the line.

Allen had just one more single-digit performance, playing against Utah with the flu.

But 20 or more points became a default. He came up big in several games scoring 28 points each in two wins against NC State, 30 points against Wake Forest, seven 3-pointers against Georgia Tech, and nailing a buzzer-beater against Virginia.

Allen is a physical basket attacker and paid a price for that, going to the foul line 252 times in 2016 and getting into several physical altercations with opponents.

He was voted first-team All-ACC and consensus second-team All-America, leading Duke to the 2016 Sweet Sixteen.

18. Obviously this is a subjective question. But few would argue with the choice of Billy King, whose shut-down of Temple's Mark Macon in the 1988 East Region title game has become the stuff of legend.

At 6-foot-6, strong and athletic, Billy King was a great defender. He was National Defensive Player of the Year in 1988.

"It started when I was a freshman and I realized playing defense was the only way I was going to get any minutes," King said in 1988. "And when your reputation is on defense, you have to be ready for people to come at you."

Many thought he was overmatched that March afternoon. Top-ranked Temple was 32-1, the only loss 59-58 to UNLV. They were led by freshman superstar Mark Macon, a 6-foot-4 All-America player already being compared to people like Oscar Robertson.

King was up for the challenge.

"I saw some tendencies I thought I could exploit," King told me later. "Macon always wanted to shoot off the dribble and he preferred to go to his left. My goal was to make him uncomfortable, to make him go places he didn't want to go."

King had help, of course. Duke switched on screens and Kevin Strickland, Robert Brickey, and Quin Snyder all had their chances with Macon.

But King was the main man. Temple had one eight-minute scoreless stretch. They kept going to Macon and kept coming up empty. Macon shot eight air balls on the way to a six for 29 horror show.

Losing coach John Chaney conceded the obvious. "They play man-to-man defense better than anybody in the country."

The final was 63-53 and Mike Krzyzewski had his second Final Four.

19. Zero, against North Carolina, on February 24, 1979. Duke won the game 47-40 after withstanding a first-half freeze by the Tar Heels.

Duke and North Carolina were the ACC's two best teams in 1979. Their first game that season took place on December 2, 1978, in the Big Four Tournament. Duke won the non-conference contest 78-68.

The Tar Heels defeated Duke in a regular-season game in Chapel Hill, 74-68, and took a one-game lead into the regular-season finale, at Duke.

There were only seven teams in the ACC that season, meaning the regular-season champions earned a first-round bye in the ACC Tournament.

Not that Duke and North Carolina needed any extra incentive.

Duke had five seniors making their final appearance in Cameron—four reserves and All-America guard Jim Spanarkel.

Center Mike Gminski, forwards Gene Banks and Kenny Dennard, and point guard Bob Bender joined Spanarkel in Duke's starting lineup.

All-America forward Mike O'Koren and defensive ace Dudley Bradley led North Carolina.

Duke entered the game ranked sixth in the AP poll; North Carolina was fourth.

The Blue Devils controlled the opening tap, missing but ultimately scoring on the offensive rebound.

Then, the fun started. North Carolina's coach Dean Smith was famous for a delay game he called the four corners. In the execution of this strategy, four players, each in a corner, with a playmaker in the middle, were ready and able to exploit any weaknesses he could find.

Smith always maintained that the four corners was not a stall tactic but rather one designed to pull a defense away from the basket and get behind it for easy layups.

Which was true. If the defense elected to come out and chase.

If it didn't? There was no shot clock in those days, and rules designed to encourage a faster pace of play—such as requiring the offense to periodically get the ball inside a certain line—were easily thwarted if both teams were so inclined.

Both teams were so inclined. North Carolina held the ball, while Bill Foster's Blue Devils stayed back in a 2-3 zone. One minute became two minutes, two became five, five became 10. After about 11 minutes of the four corners, Duke deflected a pass out of bounds, temporarily breaking the boredom.

North Carolina inbounded and burned two more minutes before Duke's defense jumped Rich Yonakor, a 6-foot-9 forward. Spanarkel came up with a steal.

Banks missed the shot, but Gminski grabbed the rebound. Yonakor fouled Gminski, who made the second of two foul shots.

It was 3-0, with 5:43 left in the half.

More cat-and-mouse ensued. The ball found its way into the hands of Yonakor, who thought it was time to shake things up a bit.

Yonakor launched a flat-footed set shot from about 19 feet out.

It missed . . . everything, including the rim and the backboard.

Duke got the rebound and finished its third possession of the game with a Gminski dunk.

North Carolina tried to hold for the final shot, but Duke again challenged Yonakor and again forced a turnover.

Spanarkel hit a layup. The Tar Heels pushed it to mid-court, where Dave Colescott missed a desperation shot.

The half ended with Duke ahead 7-0. North Carolina went 0-2 from the field and committed two turnovers in 20 minutes of "action."

Smith said afterwards that he had always planned on holding the ball for the first half, enough to take the edge off the crowd.

There was no reason to disbelieve him. But it should be noted that his team's seven-point deficit forced his hand. A scoreless second half would have resulted in a seven-point Duke win.

So, he played it straight for the final 20 minutes. Duke nursed its lead, reaching double figures on several occasions.

It was 41-32, with 30 seconds left, when Gminski grabbed an offensive rebound. Gminski was fouled but kept playing hard and was called for a technical foul for elbowing UNC's Al Wood.

Gminski was ejected.

Foster replaced Gminski with Steve Gray, who made both foul shots. O'Koren made the technical foul shots for the visitors, but Duke maintained its composure and held on for a 47-40 win.

The game is also remembered for another reason. Every time Yonakor touched the ball in the second half, the Duke students chanted "air ball," referring to his first-half brick that hit only air.

The now iconic chant may not have been invented that night. But it certainly became popularized that night.

Spanarkel led everyone with 17 points, hitting eight of nine field-goal attempts.

Years later, Spanarkel remained puzzled at Smith's strategy.

"This was a strategy you used if you thought you couldn't win. They had a great team and I don't understand why they wouldn't come in with the attitude that they could play with anybody. It was two powerhouses but only one powerhouse wanted to play."

Things didn't go well for Duke after that. The ACC regular season ended with Duke and North Carolina tied for first place. A coin toss decided the tournament bye. North Carolina won the coin toss.

Duke won two close games in the ACC Tournament but then lost Bender for the season due to an appendectomy and subsequently fell in the championship game to North Carolina.

After that, Duke lost Dennard for the season with a sprained ankle. The short-handed Blue Devils fell to St. John's 80-78 in their NCAA opener.

But the memory of "air ball" lingers.

20. Seth Curry, in 2013. Curry missed about 75 percent of Duke's practices that season and underwent surgery on his right shin a few weeks after the end of the season. Yet he still led Duke in scoring that year.

Curry is a member of America's most famous family of shooters. His father Dell made 1,245 3-pointers in 16 NBA seasons. His older brother Stephen—well, if you have to ask, you probably need to get out more.

Still, Seth was lightly recruited out of Charlotte Christian School and ended up at Liberty University, where he averaged just over 20 points per game in 2009, the nation's leading freshman scorer.

Duke lost guard Elliott Williams to transfer after the 2009 season, about the same time that Curry decided he was ready to move up a step in the competitive class.

The 6-foot-2 Curry transferred to Duke and had to sit out the 2010 season.

Curry took a starting spot in 2011 when Kyrie Irving went out with a toe injury. He had 22 points as Duke overcame a 14-point halftime deficit in defeating North Carolina and ended the season averaging nine points per game.

Duke lost Irving to NBA early-entry and Nolan Smith to graduation after the 2011 season. Curry averaged 13.2 points per game in 2012 and led Duke with a modest 2.4 assists per game, while being voted third-team All-ACC.

Curry, Mason Plumlee, and Ryan Kelly were senior starters in 2013, for a Duke team that won its first 15 games and spent the entire season in the top 10.

Curry was a vital part of this success. With sophomore Quinn Cook taking over at point guard, Curry was playing his natural position at wing and became one of the nation's top long-range bombers, while scoring off the dribble and in transition. He hit four of seven 3-pointers in a 31-point game against Santa Clara, five 3-pointers against NC State, and six of seven against Georgia Tech.

He was doing this while playing in pain and missing most practices. Curry walked in a boot, worked out on an underwater treadmill, and kept suiting up and torching ACC defenders.

"I have nothing to compare it to," Mike Krzyzewski said late in the season. "All that I know is in the middle of September, we were told that he might not be able to play this year. His parents and Seth and our medical people took a course of action to really attack the injury and come up with a plan and a test and then move along. It's incredible, really."

For his part, Curry credited his teammates for trusting him to miss practice but still keep up with assignments.

Curry scored 84 points in four NCAA Tournament games that season, as Duke advanced to the Elite Eight, before losing to Louisville. His 29-point (six for nine on 3s) performance against Michigan State in the Sweet Sixteen might have been the best game of his career.

"Seth was just at a different level than anyone else on the court offensively tonight," Krzyzewski said following that game. "To get 29 points in a game like this against a good team is just incredible."

"I feel like every time I take a shot it's going to go down, and nothing felt different tonight," Curry said.

Curry ended the season leading Duke with 17.5 points per game, making 44 percent of his 3-pointers and 81 percent of his foul shots.

He was voted second-team All-ACC by the media, first-team by the coaches. The *Sporting News* magazine named him second-team All-America, while AP named him honorable mention.

Curry missed only one game and averaged 32 minutes in the 35 games he did play.

He had surgery in mid-April that sidelined him for almost three months.

21. Steve Wojciechowski, who finished his playing career in 1998. A tough, pugnacious point guard, Wojo was universally loved by Duke partisans and universally not-loved by fans of other programs.

Wojciechowski is 5-foot-11, not blessed with great athleticism or shooting ability. He averaged 5.4 points per game at Duke and his career scoring high was 18 points.

Yet, he leveraged a high basketball IQ and a fierce tenacity into a career that saw him twice named All-ACC and the 1998 National Defensive Player of the Year. Wojo led Duke in assists and steals in 1997 and 1998 and has the second best assist to turnover ratio in Duke history.

His final home game was nationally telecast, against UNC. Wojo was named player of the game while scoring only one point. But his 11 assists and fierce defense enabled Duke to overcome a 17-point second-half deficit.

Mike Krzyzewski told the media after the game that he wanted Wojo in his foxhole.

22. Jay Buckley started at center for Duke's first two Final Four teams, in 1963 and 1964. His son Clay was a backup center on four Final Four teams, including Duke's first NCAA championship team in 1991.

Jay Buckley grew up in the D.C. suburb of Cheverly, Maryland, during a childhood that blended academics and athletics. He said he was the kind of kid who would take a board game and make the rules more complicated.

He also was six feet tall at age 12, the year he began playing organized basketball.

Buckley turned down Michigan, Vanderbilt, Virginia, and a host of Ivy League schools to attend Duke.

"I didn't think I'd feel comfortable in the Ivy League," Buckley said. "I wasn't an Ivy League type. [Duke] had the right blend of academics and basketball."

After a season on the 1961 freshman squad, Buckley joined a loaded 1962 team, led by classmate Jeff Mullins and junior Art Heyman. Buckley was a spot starter as a sophomore, averaging just under seven points and six rebounds per game.

By his junior season Buckley had put on some weight and developed a good, old-fashioned sweeping hook shot, effective with either hand.

According to Vic Bubas, he was a standout defender. "He didn't block a lot of shots, but he intimidated a lot of shots, affected a lot of shots," Bubas said. "He had a knack for being in the right place."

In 1963, Buckley became the interior anchor that enabled Heyman and Mullins to play all over the court. Buckley averaged 11 points and 10 rebounds per game, while shooting 60 percent from the field.

Buckley's game peaked in the postseason, when he became an elite rebounder. Duke went 14-0 in the 1963 ACC but still had to capture the ACC Tournament to advance to the NCAAs.

Buckley pulled down 19 rebounds in the ACC Tournament opener, against Virginia, and followed with 14 against NC State and six in the title win over Wake Forest.

He continued to rule the glass in the NCAAs, grabbing 16 rebounds in a win against NYU and 18 in the East title game against St. Joseph's.

Duke's NCAA wins sent them to Louisville. Duke was matched with Loyola of Chicago in a tight game until Heyman fouled out and Loyola pulled away.

Buckley ended that game with 10 points and 13 rebounds. That gave him 86 rebounds in Duke's first six postseason games and 14.3 rebounds per game in elimination games.

Duke returned three starters for 1964, including Mullins and Buckley. Buckley, a senior, was the leading returning rebounder and second-leading returning scorer.

He said he wasn't ready for the added responsibility. Duke went to Ann Arbor in mid-December and got hammered, 83-67, as Michigan's burly big men abused Buckley and teammate Hack Tison.

Michigan outrebounded Duke 61-35.

One local newspaper called Buckley Duke's "weak link" and his bemused teammates jokingly called him "Link" the rest of the season.

"It was a wake-up call. I did a lot of growing up. I realized I had to carry more of the load," he explained.

Buckley picked it up, scoring a career-high 26 points in a 72-71 loss at Wake Forest (Duke's only ACC loss over a two-season stretch) and 16 points and 14 rebounds against North Carolina's Billy Cunningham in a 104-69 win.

Again Duke had to run the ACC Tournament gauntlet, and again Buckley was a key component in three wins, scoring 21 points against NC State, 20 against North Carolina, and 18 points and 18 rebounds against Wake Forest.

Duke defeated Villanova and Connecticut to win the East.

Buckley had a total of 21 points and 18 rebounds in the victories.

The 1964 Final Four took place in Kansas City. Duke's next opponent was Michigan, the same Michigan that had bludgeoned them earlier in the season.

Buckley was primed for the rematch. He wrapped himself around Bill Buntin, a 6-foot-7, 240-pound All-America player, and had the best game of his career. Buckley made 11 of 16 from the field, outscored Buntin 25-19, and outrebounded him 14-9.

Duke won 91-80 and advanced to the NCAA title game.

Undefeated and top-ranked UCLA was left. Duke played well for most of the game. But a brief lapse late in the first half did them in. A 15-0 run turned a three-point Duke lead into a 12-point deficit. Duke couldn't catch up and fell 98-83 in what was John Wooden's first national title.

Buckley ended his playing career with an 18-point, nine-rebound performance.

He averaged 14 points and nine rebounds for the season and was selected second-team All-ACC.

The Los Angeles Lakers drafted Buckley, but given his success in academics—especially in the sciences—he had other options aside from playing basketball. In fact, Buckley, an Academic All-America player, was so smart that Bubas jokes that he ordered Buckley not to talk during timeouts because "he would confuse us."

Buckley had spent the summers of 1962 and 1963 interning with NASA but realized that his height ruled out being an astronaut. He ultimately graduated from Duke with a degree in physics and accepted an offer from Johns Hopkins University for a National Science Foundation Fellowship. Buckley figured the value of the scholarship was more than anything he could earn as a back-up NBA center. At Hopkins, he earned a doctorate in physics/atmospheric sciences.

Buckley worked with a variety of space-related firms, including Ball Aerospace and the space division of General Electric, specializing in satellites.

Like his father, a 6-foot-10 post player, Clay Buckley was bothered by chronic back issues and never became a rotation player. He scored 148 points in four seasons, all of which ended in the Final Four.

Clay saw action in the 1989 and 1990 Final Fours.

Jay's younger brother—and Clay's uncle—Bruce Buckley was a key reserve on North Carolina's 1977 team, which lost to Marquette in the title game.

23. Danny Ferry led Duke with 14.0 points, 7.8 rebounds, and 4.3 assists in 1987, his sophomore season. Ferry built on that to become an All-America player in his final two seasons.

The 6-foot-10 Ferry had a rare hoops background. His father Bob played 10 seasons in the NBA and then became a general manager, winning the NBA General Manager of the Year award twice. Older brother Bob Ferry Jr. played at Harvard. Danny prepped at fabled DeMatha High School, under the tutelage of equally fabled Morgan Wooten.

"I grew up dreaming of playing in the NBA," Ferry said years later. "I was more of an NBA fan growing up. After all, the NBA was my babysitter 41 nights a year."

Ferry was the nation's top-ranked prep player in 1985 and picked Duke over North Carolina and Maryland, the first recruit to turn down Dean Smith for Mike Krzyzewski.

"I just had a connection with Krzyzewski. He pulled me there like a magnet," Ferry said. "I could hear his vision. Once I met the players, I knew Duke was the place for me."

Ferry was a complementary player as a freshman on a team that started four seniors and went 37-3, losing to Louisville in the title game.

The 1987 season was a crucial one for Krzyzewski, who was trying to demonstrate that he was putting together a great program, not just a great team. Ferry and senior point guard Tommy Amaker were the key returnees from 1986 and Krzyzewski built the 1987 team around them.

The media picked Duke sixth in the ACC that season and Duke didn't crack the AP top-25 until the end of December, after starting 11-1.

Krzyzewski turned Ferry loose. "He didn't have a position and played everything for us, including point guard," Krzyzewski told me later. "He loved to pass more than any other aspect of his game, which again shows the type of team player he was."

Ferry stuffed many a stat sheet, approaching a triple-double at Maryland, with 20 points, 19 rebounds, and seven assists in an 85-61 win. In a win over NC State, he tallied 10 points, five rebounds, and eight assists.

Duke ended the 1987 season in the Sweet Sixteen. Duke's 24-9 mark solidified the program.

Ferry elevated his game in 1988. "Mike Krzyzewski empowered me," he recalled. "He built me up. I had an unbelievable level of confidence, an unbelievable level of freedom."

Krzyzewski agreed. "You coach players differently who have the emotional makeup and the ability to be great. You allow them to follow their instincts. We did that with Danny and we benefitted immensely from that."

Ferry became the best player in the ACC. He had 33 points in a win over Maryland and 29 against Wake Forest. Duke swept North Carolina in the regular season and beat them in the ACC Tournament title game, Duke's first 3-0 sweep of the Tar Heels since 1966.

Ferry won the Everett Case Award presented to the tournament's top player. He scored 70 points, with 34 rebounds, in four East Region games, including a game-high 20 in a 63-53 upset over top-ranked Temple in the title game.

Duke fell behind Kansas 24-6 in the Final Four. Ferry led a comeback that cut the deficit to two before running out of gas. Ferry scored 19, but Kansas won the game 66-59 and defeated Oklahoma two days later for the title.

Ferry led the ACC with 19.1 points per game and added 7.6 rebounds, 4.0 assists, 1.3 steals, and 0.7 blocks per game. He was named ACC Player of the Year, Krzyzewski's first.

Duke began the 1988-89 season ranked number one in the AP poll. Ferry was joined by junior Alaa Abdelnaby and freshman Christian Laettner, giving Duke three players 6-foot-10 or taller who would be first-round NBA draft picks.

This gave Ferry more freedom to play on the perimeter, a freedom he exploited with a career-best 45 successful 3-pointers (42.5 percent).

Duke started 13-0 before losing three straight conference games. Ferry struggled through some back problems but was playing as well as any player in the country down the stretch, tallying 28 points, eight rebounds, and six assists against Notre Dame; 24 points and nine assists against Virginia; and 26 points and 10 rebounds against Kansas. Ferry outscored Arizona's All-America forward Sean Elliott 29-24 in a 77-75 Arizona win in the Meadowlands.

Duke finished second in the ACC and lost 77-74 to North Carolina in the ACC Tournament championship game. Ferry scored 14 points and added seven assists.

Duke was seeded second in the East. Wins over South Carolina State, West Virginia, and Minnesota advanced Duke to the East finals, against top-seeded Georgetown.

Duke knocked off the Hoyas 85-77, with Laettner outplaying fellow freshman Alonzo Mourning and Ferry putting up a 21-point, seven-rebound, three-assist stat line.

Ferry was named the East Regional Most Outstanding Player.

The ninth-ranked Blue Devils squared off against 11th-ranked Seton Hall in the Final Four. Duke jumped to a 26-8 lead but lost starting forward Robert Brickey to a knee injury and fell apart.

Ferry scored 34 points but didn't get much help, as Seton Hall pulled away down the stretch for a 95-78 win.

Ferry ended the season with a 22.6 points-per-game average. Only J.J. Redick in 2006 has bettered that during Mike Krzyzewski's tenure at Duke. Ferry repeated as the ACC Player of the Year, the first Duke player to win twice; only Redick has matched that.

Ferry and Elliott split the National Player of the Year awards, with Ferry winning the UPI, Naismith, and USBWA. He finished his Duke career with 2,155 points, 1,003 rebounds, and 506 assists, all of which are still in the top 10 at Duke.

Krzyzewski calls Ferry a bridge. "During his junior and senior years, Danny was a great player. He taught our system and culture to our young guys."

24. Duke's Tommy Amaker, in 1987. The award was started that year by the National Association of Basketball Coaches.

Tommy Amaker was a four-year starter at point guard and averaged six assists per game for Mike Krzyzewski's first great team, in 1986.

Amaker relied on quickness and guile to become a great defender.

Mark Alarie, his teammate for three seasons, explained why Amaker was so successful. "He could apply so much pressure on the other team's point guard that he prevented other teams from running their offense."

Tommy Amaker grabs the loose ball in Duke's 74-73 loss to Boston College in the 1985 NCAA Tournament. (AP Photo/Ron Heflin)

Amaker was a senior in 1987, when Duke might have had its best ever defensive team. Led by Amaker and wings Billy King and Kevin Strickland, Duke forced 20 turnovers a game and held opponents to 45 percent shooting and 67 points per game.

Amaker led that team with 58 steals, while adding 12 points and four assists to the ledger.

He ranks third in career steals at Duke, with 259, and set a Final Four record with seven steals against Louisville in 1986.

25. Nolan Smith starred for Duke's 2010 NCAA champions. His father Derek Smith likewise starred for Louisville's 1980 NCAA champions. Tragically, Derek Smith did not live to see his son's success, dying of a heart attack in 1996, at the age of 35.

Nolan Smith is one of 13 Duke players to be voted ACC Player of the Year, and he may have come the longest distance. He struggled much of his first two seasons at Duke, bothered by inconsistency, knee problems, and a concussion suffered when he ran into a screen at Maryland in 2009.

Smith put it together as a junior in 2010, averaging 17 points and three assists, while guarding the opposition's top perimeter scorer. A late tie-breaking 3-pointer was the biggest play of Duke's Elite Eight win over Baylor.

He led Duke with 29 points in the Baylor game.

Smith scored 32 points in the Final Four, as Duke captured its fourth NCAA title.

He peaked as a senior, blending in with talented freshman guard Kyrie Irving early in the season and then taking over the team once Irving went down with a toe injury. His career-high 34 points came at home against North Carolina, helping Duke overcome a 16-point deficit for a 79-73 win.

"This comeback win, how tough we were, how together we were and how great it feels now, I don't think anything can be better than this," Smith said.

Smith won the Everett Case Award as Duke captured the ACC Tournament title and led Duke into the Sweet Sixteen with a game-high 24 points in a 73-71 win over Michigan.

In addition to his ACC honors, Smith was unanimous first-team All-America.

26. Mike Lewis, in 1966 and 1968. A native of Missoula, Montana, Lewis was Vic Bubas's best center and one of the best rebounders in ACC history.

It's easy to think of Lewis as some kind of rustic mountain man, barely acquainted with indoor plumbing or electricity.

The reality was much different. Lewis went to a high school with 2,000 students and his high school coach, Lou Rocheleau, had been a star center at the University of Montana. Lewis claims that his high school big-man drills were more sophisticated than what Duke was doing when he arrived in Durham.

Why come all the way across the country? "I had a great visit," Lewis explained. "I liked the coaches. I liked the campus. I wanted to go away from home. I could have gone to UCLA. I'm not sure I can explain it. But something about Duke just grabbed me."

Lewis joined a loaded team in 1966, starting from day one at center, alongside forwards Jack Marin and Bob Riedy and guards Steve Vacendak and Bob Verga, the first ever Duke starting lineup in which all five starters were future pros.

Lewis provided a strong interior presence, giving Duke 14 points and 11 rebounds per game. His free throw with seconds left gave Duke a 21-20 win over North Carolina in the ACC Tournament semifinals.

Lewis grabbed 14 rebounds the following day as Duke defeated NC State 71-66 to win the ACC Tournament.

Lewis had a solid East Regional Tournament as well, capturing 30 points and 28 rebounds in wins over St. Joseph's and Syracuse.

Verga was sick in the Final Four and Duke lost to Kentucky, 83-79. Lewis had 21 points but only six rebounds. "Kentucky didn't have much size," he said. "I should have scored more. I'm not sure we could have beaten Texas Western the next night, but I would have liked a chance to try."

Texas Western beat Kentucky for the title, while Duke defeated Utah in the consolation game.

It would be Duke's last NCAA Tournament game for 12 years.

Lewis improved his scoring and rebounding as a junior. But Duke struggled to an 18-9 record, including two early-season blowout road losses to UCLA and their sophomore phenom Lew Alcindor.

Lewis said the unsuccessful road trip demoralized Duke and they never recovered.

All of the stars were gone in 1968 except Lewis, who put together one of the best individual Duke seasons of the decade.

"This was a bunch of guys who got along great," he said. "The game was fun again."

Lewis was the focal point of the offense, averaging 21.7 points per game. He had 32 points in a 93-72 win over Michigan and Rudy Tomjanovich; 33 points in a win over Princeton, a career-high 35 points against Wake Forest; 34 points and 22 rebounds against NC State; and 32 points and 18 rebounds against Maryland, all in wins.

His 14.4 rebounds per game not only led the ACC but remains the top single-season Duke mark during the team's ACC tenure.

Duke finished second in the ACC behind North Carolina, splitting two games in the regular season. The eagerly anticipated rubber match never took place as Duke lost to NC State in the ACC Tournament, 12-10, victims of arguably the most notorious slow-down in college basketball history.

Duke got a bid to the NIT, defeated Oklahoma City—the first NIT win by any ACC school—and then lost to hometown St. Peter's, as Lewis fouled out, barely breaking a sweat.

Lewis ended his Duke career with averages of 16.9 points and 12.5 rebounds. His rebounding average remains the second highest in Duke history.

27. Kyle Singler played 4,887 minutes for Duke in a career that ended in 2011. He maximized those minutes, scoring 2,392 points (4th), grabbing 1,015 rebounds (7th) and making 267 3-pointers (5th) over the course of his Duke career.

Singler was a remarkably consistent and reliable player. He never missed a game at Duke, shrugging off injuries that would have sidelined others. He and Christian Laettner are tied at the top of the list in games played at Duke, with 148. He started all but one of those—Mike Krzyzewski benched all of the starters one time to make a point—and Duke won 125.

Singler is 6-foot-8 and played all over the frontcourt. He was ACC Freshman of the Year in 2008 and made All-ACC four times, including first team in 2010 and 2011.

His career highlight was the 2010 NCAA Tournament. He overcame an 0-10 shooting performance against Baylor in the Elite Eight to score 40 points in the Final Four, leading to Duke's fourth NCAA title and a Most Outstanding Player Award.

After Singler's final home game, Krzyzewski tried to sum him up.

"Kyle has been . . . you know, what position does he play, he plays 'winner.' Ok I'm going to pick a team. Ok I pick you because I want to win. . . . Kyle has been the prime guy for that for four years."

3

THREE-POINTER LEVEL

1. How many times have Duke and North Carolina met in the postseason? *Answer on page 177.*

2. When did Duke play its first basketball game? *Answer on page 178.*

3. Who holds the Duke record for steals in one game? *Answer on page 180.*

4. How many three-time first-team All-ACC players has Mike Krzyzewski had at Duke? *Answer on page 182.*

5. Who was named ACC Player of the Year in the same year they weren't voted first-team All-ACC? *Answer on page 185.*

6. What is the biggest deficit overcome by a winning college team? *Answer on page 188.*

7. When did Duke post its first victory over a No. 1 team? *Answer on page 189.*

8. Who was the 16-term congressman who played for Duke? *Answer on page 190.*

9. What was the "Mongoose"? *Answer on page 190.*

10. Who was the Duke basketball player who spent part of World War II as a German POW? *Answer on page 191.*

11. Mike Krzyzewski's first NCAA Tournament team included a starter who gave up hockey for hoops. Who was that player? *Answer on page 192.*

12. Which Duke athlete was an All-America player in both basketball and lacrosse? *Answer on page 192.*

13. What is the most points ever scored by Duke in a single game? *Answer on page 194.*

14. What was the first ACC team to play in the NIT? *Answer on page 194.*

15. Who was Duke's first NBA player? *Answer on page 196.*

16. Who was Duke's first basketball All-America player? *Answer on page 197.*

17. What is the longest game that Duke has ever played? *Answer on page 198.*

18. Who was Duke's first African American basketball player? *Answer on page 202.*

19. Who had the best rebounding season in Duke history? *Answer on page 204.*

20. Who coached Duke to its first appearance in the NCAA Tournament? *Answer on page 205.*

21. Who was the first person to play in four Final Fours? *Answer on page 209.*

22. What happened to Duke's starting lineup in its first game of the 1967 calendar year? *Answer on page 210.*

23. How many triple-doubles has Duke had? *Answer on page 211.*

24. Which Duke player's father was a U.S. Olympic medalist in track and field? *Answer on page 212.*

25. Why did Duke only play 12 ACC games in 1967? *Answer on page 213.*

26. What was the first team to have three first-team All-ACC players? *Answer on page 214.*

27. Why is Robby West a Duke hero? *Answer on page 215.*

28. Which Duke basketball star won the Punt, Pass and Kick contest? *Answer on page 217.*

29. Who scored 33 points for Duke while playing with a broken wrist? *Answer on page 220.*

30. Who was the Duke soccer coach who became the head basketball coach? *Answer on page 222.*

31. Who is the only person to play for different teams in the Final Four? *Answer on page 225.*

32. Mike Krzyzewski has accepted five transfers.

Match them with their previous school.

1. Roshown McLeod

2. Dahntay Jones

3. Seth Curry

4. Rodney Hood

5. Sean Obi

    A. Liberty

    B. Mississippi State

    C. Rice

    D. Rutgers

    E. St. John's

Answer on page 226.

THREE-POINTER –
ANSWERS

1. Only once. North Carolina edged Duke 73-67 in the 1971 NIT, held in Madison Square Garden. The match was in the semifinals. North Carolina defeated Georgia Tech two days later to become the first ACC team to win the NIT.

The NIT meant more in those days, when only one team per conference could advance to the NCAAs. North Carolina actually won the ACC regular season that year but lost in the tournament title game to South Carolina at the buzzer.

The 1971 team was the best of Bucky Waters's four teams at Duke, a veteran squad led by senior center Randy Denton. Duke defeated Dayton and Tennessee in its first two NIT games to go to 20-8. This would be Duke's only 20-win team between 1968 and 1978.

Duke and Carolina had already met three times, with North Carolina winning in the Big Four and each team winning at home in the ACC.

Duke got off to a horrible start in the 1971 NIT, missing its first four shots and committing five turnovers before getting on the board five minutes into the game, already down 9-2.

Duke closed to 19-18, fell behind 31-20, and closed it to 31-26 at intermission.

Carolina made the decisive move with 13 minutes left, a 10-0 run that put them up 53-39.

Duke got as close as 56-51, but Denton fouled out with 5:32 left. North Carolina scored its last 17 points from the foul line.

Richie O'Connor led Duke with 18 as foul-plagued Denton was held to 10 points and nine rebounds.

"They outquicked us," Waters said after the game. "We were very tight early."

Duke and North Carolina have had two tantalizing NCAA near-misses. In 1979 they were seeded to meet in the East Region title game in Greensboro.

But both lost their opening game, in nearby Raleigh.

The two schools advanced to the 1991 Final Four. But North Carolina lost to Kansas, ruining a potential title game with Duke.

2. In 1906. On March 2, to be exact. Duke University was still Trinity College in those days. Trinity's first opponent was Wake Forest College, then located in the town of Wake Forest, about 20 miles north of Raleigh and 40 miles east of Durham.

This was five years before the University of North Carolina and North Carolina State began intercollegiate play.

Of course, NC State was North Carolina A&M at the time.

In other words, a long time ago, and pretty early in the game itself. In fact, basketball was barely a decade old at that point. Wake Forest and Guilford participated in the first college game ever played in the South just a few weeks before Wake and Trinity met. The teams met again a second time that year.

Wake Forest won both games against Trinity, by scores of 24-10 and 15-5.

Later that season, Trinity won two of three games against a local high school.

Yes, Duke/Trinity's first team actually lost a game to Trinity Park High School.

Trinity's first coach was Wilbur "Cap" Card, a former star athlete at Trinity. In fact, Card got his nickname because he was the captain of the baseball team.

Card came to Trinity to become a Methodist minister before becoming smitten with athletics.

He graduated from Trinity in 1900 and turned down a chance to play professional baseball, choosing to become a physical education professional at a time when that profession was in its infancy.

Card studied at Harvard's Sargent Normal School of Physical Education, graduating in 1902 and returning every summer for additional training.

Card introduced basketball to his P.E. classes in 1905, two years after he started Trinity's track and field team.

Card was friends with his Wake Forest contemporary, Richard Crozier. Crozier invited Card to a friendly game of hoops. Card had three weeks to hold practices for his team, none of whom had ever played a basketball game.

Since few people were familiar with the rules, Card and Crozier officiated.

If Trinity was one of the first schools to dip its toes in the water, it did little more than that for a generation. Card stayed on the staff until 1943 but only coached for seven seasons and was never paid a penny for his basketball endeavors.

Card's win-loss record was 30-17, with 10 games against YMCAs and nine against high schools. Duke beat Littleton High School 62-1 in 1907 and lost to the same school 11-3 the following season.

Trinity scheduled games against local YMCAs as late as 1927. The games against high schools just show how unstructured the new game was in the early days. Trinity didn't play any high schools after 1909.

But those high schools started sending experienced players to colleges and once teams had players who weren't learning on the spot, the quality improved dramatically.

J.E. Brin, who had played for Card and graduated from Trinity in 1911, replaced Card as coach in 1912. Trinity started playing more games but ran through 10 coaches from 1912 until 1928, when Duke got serious about basketball.

By our standards, these early games would have been a chore to watch. Who among us would willingly subject ourselves to an 11-3 contest?

But it looked a lot different to turn-of-the-century eyes. In 1906, the *Trinity Chronicle*, the school newspaper, praised those first games as "one of the most fascinating and most intensely interesting indoor sports known today."

We might not recognize the game, but we certainly recognize fascination, intensity, and interest.

Card Gym is located a hop, skip, and a jump away from Cameron Indoor Stadium on Duke's West Campus. Opened in 1930, the facility served as Duke's home court for a decade. Originally called the Duke Gym, it was renamed Card Gym in 1958, 10 years after Card's death. It is still heavily used for intramural competition, a fitting use for a facility named after Duke's first physical education professional.

3. Kenny Dennard had 11 steals February 3, 1979, against Maryland. The game, which Duke won 87-78, was played at Cameron Indoor Stadium. Dennard scored 13 points for the Blue Devils.

A school record in steals but only 13 points? That was typical of Dennard. His teammates at Duke included Jim

Spanarkel, Mike Gminski, Gene Banks, and Vince Taylor. He was never the best player on the team and he never made All-ACC.

But Dennard helped Duke win basketball games. A 6-foot-8 forward from the small town of King, North Carolina, Dennard came to Duke at the same time as Banks. The two were both about 6-foot-8, 220 pounds and served as bookend forwards.

Dennard was the only player Bill Foster recruited from a North Carolina high school. He was one of those guys who set screens, blocked out on the boards, dug out loose balls, and looked for targets of opportunity around the basket.

Which isn't to say that he couldn't light it up. When Clemson decided to shut down Gminski in the 1978 ACC Tournament, they left open Dennard, who knocked down 10 of 14 from the field and led everyone with 22 points.

Dennard scored 41 points and grabbed 29 rebounds in Duke's five-game run to the 1978 title game. Sixteen of those points came during the East Region championship win over Villanova.

By this point Dennard was known as much for his exuberant personality as his on-court abilities.

Dennard punctuated that Villanova win with a reverse dunk in transition, after which he proclaimed it the first such nationally telecast reverse dunk.

His teammates nicknamed him "Crash."

Dennard's impulsiveness didn't always serve him well though. In March 1979 he decided to play in an impromptu pick-up game and suffered an ankle sprain that kept him out of Duke's NCAA Tournament opener. Duke lost to St. John's 80-78.

Dennard also missed nine games with a deep thigh bruise in 1980, but he recovered in time to help Duke win the ACC Tournament, contributing 28 points and 14 rebounds in three wins.

Foster left for South Carolina after the 1980 season and was replaced by 33-year-old Army coach Mike Krzyzewski.

Dennard recalled first hearing about Coach K. "This was before ESPN, before the Internet. It was like Pony Express. I saw something in *USA Today* and thought 'hmm.' We didn't know who he was, what he was going to do."

Duke made the NIT that season.

Dennard went out with both barrels blazing. Duke hosted North Carolina A&T in the NIT opener and Banks went down with a broken wrist.

Duke won 79-69 but few gave them much of a chance in the second round, with Alabama up next and Banks on the sideline.

Dennard rose to the occasion with perhaps the best game of his career, in which he collected 23 points and 10 rebounds, leading Duke to a 75-70 win. A career 59 percent foul shooter, Dennard said farewell to Cameron with an 11-12 effort from the line.

Duke went to West Lafayette to play Purdue, the team that had ended the Blue Devils' 1980 season. The outcome was the same this time around, an 81-69 Purdue victory. Dennard had nine points and a team-high nine rebounds.

Dennard wasn't the greatest Duke player of his generation, but he might be the most fondly remembered. His sheer love of the game and of life remains a vivid memory for anyone who saw him play.

4. Only one—shooting guard Trajan Langdon, in 1997, 1998, and 1999. Duke won 93 games in those three seasons.

Langdon came to Duke from Anchorage, Alaska and was known as the "Alaskan Assassin."

Anchorage may seem pretty isolated from the basketball mainstream. But Langdon played summer AAU ball in the lower 48 and was a consensus top-10 recruit and a McDonald's All-America player.

Langdon's first love was baseball and he actually played minor league ball in the San Diego Padres system over the summer while attending Duke. But he was never able to overcome the disadvantage of the short Alaskan baseball season.

Langdon came down to Duke and Stanford for visits.

"Duke and Stanford were a wash academically. Duke had a good basketball history, a chance to showcase my skills, and the coaching to help me improve. Coach K was huge, the ACC was better than the Pac-10, and Duke was on national TV, which made it possible for my family and friends to watch me play."

The 6-foot-3 Langdon came to Duke with two other McDonald's All-America athletes, point guard Steve Wojciechowski and wing Ricky Price, as part of Duke's first class with three McDonald's All-America players.

Langdon averaged 11.3 points per game as a freshman in 1995. But Mike Krzyzewski missed much of that season following back surgery and Duke fell to 13-18.

Langdon injured an ankle over the summer, which led to knee injury, and ultimately to surgery. He missed the entire 1996 season, gaining a medical redshirt.

Duke went 18-13 that year.

Duke needed a bounce back after a 31-31 two-year run and Langdon helped them get it.

He became Duke's go-to scorer, leading the team with over 14 points per game, almost 17 per game in ACC play. He scored 28 points in an 80-73 win over North Carolina, ending a seven-game Duke losing streak to the Tar Heels.

Duke won the regular season title and Langdon ended a two-year Duke drought when he was voted first-team All-ACC.

A lack of size and rebounding doomed Duke in the NCAAs, where Duke lost to Providence in the second round.

Freshmen Elton Brand, Shane Battier, and Chris Burgess eliminated the size deficit and Duke had spectacular seasons in 1998 and 1999, a combined record of 69-6, 31-1 in the ACC regular season, two regular season titles, one ACC Tournament title, and the most wins in consecutive seasons in Duke history.

By this point Langdon was known equally for the accuracy of his long-range shooting and the imperturbable calm with which he delivered those daggers.

Some thought that Langdon's apparent disinterest signaled a lack of fire.

Wojciechowski said nothing could be further from the truth.

"No one in the program was more competitive than Trajan," Wojo explained. "He was always ready to compete and win. As hard a worker as I have been around. He was in the gym at all hours, a ball, a basket, and Trajan."

Langdon had three of the four most successful seasons from the 3-point line in Duke history when he graduated and led the ACC in free-throw percentage in 1997. He's still fourth in ACC history in made 3-pointers and ranks in the top 10 in career free throw percentage.

Langdon was consensus third-team All-America in 1998, and second-team in 1999. A math major, he also was named academic All-ACC three times.

The one thing Langdon couldn't do is will Duke to a national title. Duke made it to the 1998 Elite Eight but couldn't hold a 17-point lead and fell to Kentucky 88-86 despite Langdon's 18 points.

Duke dominated the 1999 season, taking a 37-1 record into the title game against Connecticut. Langdon had perhaps the best game of his career, collecting five 3-pointers as part of a team-high 25 points. But he was called for traveling after being tripped with Duke down by a point and five seconds left.

Connecticut got the win.

It was a brutal, bitter loss.

Trajan Langdon turns the corner against Clemson. (AP Photo/ Karl DeBlaker)

Nevertheless, the team had come a long way from Langdon's 13-18 freshman season.

"I never forgot my freshman year," he said. "The team got better and better and I got better and better. I had an understanding of my strengths. I worked hard every night, tried to be a good teammate, and competed. I wanted to be good. When my career was over, I realized how high a mountain we had climbed."

J.J. Redick has come along since then but in 1999 Mike Krzyzewski proclaimed Langdon "the best shooter I have ever had."

5. Duke's Steve Vacendak, in 1966. You have to think about this one. How can a player be the player of the year without being one of the league's five best players?

The short answer is that Vacendak had a very good week. Back in 1966 the ACC media voted for the All-ACC team following the final regular season game but didn't select the ACC Player of the Year until the conclusion of the ACC Tournament.

Vacendak was a master of doing the little things that don't always show up in the stat sheets and those little things helped Duke capture the 1966 ACC Tournament title, its fourth ACC championship in seven seasons.

Vic Bubas had to be convinced to recruit Vacendak. Vacendak was a 6-foot-1 center from Scranton and Bubas didn't have much use for 6-foot-1 centers.

However, Duke assistant coach Bucky Waters absolutely loved Vacendak's intangibles. When Bubas pressed Waters as to why Duke should recruit an ordinary athlete, with ordinary basketball skills, Waters gave a simple answer—his teams win.

Vacendak was a key reserve on Duke's 1964 NCAA runner-up team but showed his mettle the following season, averaging 16 points and 6.6 rebounds as an undersized forward in a three-guard lineup.

Vacendak was named to the 1965 All-ACC second team, as Duke went 20-5.

Vacendak moved to the point guard position as a senior.

Assist statistics weren't kept in those days, nor were steal statistics.

Had they been, Vacendak would have been among the ACC leaders, perhaps at the top.

Wake Forest coach Jack Murdock said of Vacendak, "He was a very good defensive player and the team leader. His job was to get everybody in the right place and make sure they did their jobs."

Duke finished first in the ACC regular season at 12-2. Marin and Verga were voted first team All-ACC. Vacendak was ninth in the total voting.

Clemson head coach Bobby Roberts thought Vacendak was under-valued. "How in the world could anyone pick an all-conference team and leave off Steve Vacendak of Duke? He's the heart and soul of the Duke team."

Duke had an easy win in the ACC Tournament opener.

The semifinal game was a different story. Duke faced North Carolina and Dean Smith's four corners delay offense.

Duke took a 7-5 lead into halftime but fell behind 17-13 in the second half. Vacendak hit a long jumper and forced a couple of turnovers, as Duke ramped up their defensive pressure.

Vacendak came up with a crucial loose ball and tied the game 20-20, with seconds left. Mike Lewis rebounded a miss and made a foul shot, giving Duke the 21-20 victory.

That put Duke into the title game against second-seeded North Carolina State. The Wolfpack jumped to a 19-10 lead before Vacendak led a rally that cut the State lead to a point at the half.

But Duke couldn't get over the hump and trailed 62-56, with 4:28 remaining. Vacendak hit two long jumpers and scored on an offensive rebound to give Duke a 64-63 lead. Vacendak wrapped up Duke's 71-66 victory with two foul shots, giving him 18 points, the Everett Case Award for the tournament's outstanding player, and an unlikely ACC Player of the Year award.

Vic Bubas refused to get into the controversy but did praise Vacendak as "the best battler we have had since I've been at Duke. There's no doubt in my mind who leaves the most out there all the time."

Vacendak went on to score 60 points in four games, as Duke finished third in the NCAA Tournament.

Vacendak's 13.2 points per game average in 1966 is the lowest ever for an ACC Player of the Year, and his selection can be seen as a vindication for doing the little things better than anyone else.

6. Duke came from 32 points down to defeat Tulane in the 1950 Dixie Classic, held in Reynolds Coliseum, on the campus of North Carolina State.

Tulane came into the Dixie Classic with a 3-3 record. The Green Wave lost to North Carolina State 89-75 in its first game and defeated Rhode Island 81-62.

Duke followed a similar path, losing to Colgate and defeating North Carolina.

Thus Duke and Tulane were playing for fifth place.

It was close early. Tulane led 22-19 when they exploded on a 22-0 run. During a stoppage of play, referee Arnold Heft jokingly told the scorekeeper that he might need a new basketball, "this one's so hot, I can't handle it."

Tulane's lead crested at 32 points, 54-22. Duke closed to 56-27 at halftime, but no one would have considered that much of a harbinger.

Remember, there was no shot clock and no 3-point shot in those days. Tulane had all the advantages.

But Duke had the best player on the floor.

Duke closed to 72-52, with about eight minutes to play. It was progress for Duke, but they were running out of time.

That was the point at which Dick Groat took over. He scored 12 points in a span of about five minutes.

A local newspaper summarized this Superman act, calling him "a wizard with the basketball, hitting from all angles and driving through the weary Tulane defense for basket after basket."

Tulane began to panic. They were a fast-break team. Once they started trying to hold the ball and milk the clock, the wheels started to come off. One Tulane turnover after another led to one Duke basket after another.

A Groat field goal tied the game at 72-72, with about a minute left.

Tulane turned it over again. They swarmed over Groat, which left his teammate Dayton Allen open. He scored at the buzzer, for the 74-72 win.

Tulane went the final eight minutes of the game without scoring a single point. Duke outscored Tulane 47-16 in the second half, 52-18 after Tulane took its largest lead.

Groat led everyone with 32 points, 24 in the second half.

With a shot clock and a 3-point shot, this is one record that might be made to be broken. In fact, it was almost broken in 1994 when Kentucky overcame a 31-point deficit to defeat LSU.

7. Duke defeated West Virginia 72-68 on January 27, 1958. The game was played at Duke and resulted in West Virginia's first loss of the season.

The Mountaineers had two AP All-America athletes that year, senior Lloyd Sharrar and sophomore Jerry West. West had 20 points and 14 rebounds. But Duke held Sharrar to nine points. Jim Newcombe led Duke with 20 points and 14 rebounds. Bob Vernon added 18 points.

This was the first victory over a top-ranked team by any ACC team, the ACC being in its fifth season.

8. Henry Hyde was a backup on the Georgetown team that finished second in the 1943 NCAA Tournament. After enlisting in the Navy, he was sent to Duke as a part of the V-12 program. Hyde played 25 games for Duke in 1944, scoring 53 points.

Hyde served in the Navy, got his degree from Georgetown and law degree from Loyola, and served in the Illinois legislature. He was first elected to the United States House of Representatives in 1974, representing Chicago's northwestern suburbs. He was reelected 15 times.

9. That was Bucky Waters's fanciful nickname for his spread game back in 1973. Nothing really distinguished it from other spread offenses. But a Duke coach couldn't very well call it a four corners.

Duke went 12-14 that season, after which Waters resigned when he couldn't get a contract extension.

Even the best schemes need talent.

But for one magical night that season, the Mongoose helped carry out the most effective scheme in college basketball.

Gary Melchionni was the trigger man. A 6-foot-3 lefty, Melchionni was a good player, good enough to be second-team All-ACC in 1972 and first-team in 1973.

He was a great player against third-ranked Maryland.

Maryland chased, Melchionni drove, Melchionni scored. Rinse and repeat.

In one 2:20 span in the second half, he scored 11 points on five possessions as Duke extended its lead from 66-60 to 77-62.

Melchionni ended with 39 points, having made 17-25 from the field and 5-6 from the line.

Duke won 85-81.

"Everything seemed to be dropping," he told me decades later. "Maryland never adjusted to what we were doing. I can't believe they let me score that many."

Melchionni's son Lee played at Duke from 2002 to 2006.

10. John "Bubber" Seward was captured by the Germans in the latter days of the war and spent 71 days in Stalag 2-A, near Linburg, Germany. Seward played for Duke both before and after his military service.

Seward was a 6-foot-2 forward from Newport News, Virginia. He was a key component of Duke's 1942 Southern Conference championship team and averaged 10.2 points per game the following season.

Seward joined the Army and was sent to the European theater as a member of the Seventh Army 103rd Infantry Division. His unit was captured on January 20, 1945 and kept as POWs until liberated by American forces at the end of March.

The winter of 1945 was brutally cold and POWs were poorly fed, poorly clothed, and poorly housed. Seward said that he was always cold and always hungry. He even lost 40 pounds while there.

Seward came back to Duke and led the squad to the 1946 Southern Conference title, making All–Southern Conference in the process.

He finished his Duke career in 1947, captaining Duke to a 19-8 mark.

Seward played 100 games at Duke, scoring 896 points.

Seward died in 2008, at the age of 86, 63 years after surviving the horrors of a German POW camp.

11. Dan Meagher. A native of St. Catherine's, Ontario, Meagher started at power forward for Duke's 1984 and 1985 teams, both of which advanced to the NCAA Tournament.

Kids in Canada grow up dreaming of playing in the NHL, and Meagher was one of those kids—until he discovered basketball.

"I just fell in love with hoops. It was fun. Nothing more complicated than that," he said.

Meagher never averaged more than about eight points and four rebounds per game at Duke. But at 6-foot-7, 215 pounds, he delighted fans and aggravated opponents with a take-no-prisoners approach to the game.

"My hockey background helped me," he explained. "I wasn't afraid of the competition. I didn't back down from anyone. I still take pride in being part of the teams that helped revive Duke basketball."

12. Ed Koffenberger, a 1940s athlete who didn't even play lacrosse before entering college.

A native of Wilmington, Delaware, the 6-foot-2 Koffenberger showed up at the University of North Carolina in the fall of 1944 as a member of that school's Navy V-12 program.

Koffenberger was playing football for the Tar Heels when he informed Navy officials that he wanted to become an engineer.

UNC didn't have an engineering program, but Duke did. Duke also had a V-12 program. In a matter of days, Ed Koffenberger was a Blue Devil.

"I really had no choice in the matter," he said years later. "I didn't even know that Duke had an engineering program. I thought I would be sent to Georgia Tech or somewhere up North."

Koffenberger didn't play much football and ultimately gave it up.

But it was a different story on the basketball court. He was an under-sized center who got by on quickness and guile.

The highlight of his basketball career was the 1946 Southern Conference Tournament, when he scored 16 points to lead Duke to a come-from-behind overtime win over NC State and 11 points in a 49-30 title-game victory over Wake Forest.

At 21-6 and with the conference title in hand, Duke expected an invitation to the eight-team NCAA Tournament. But the bid went to UNC, the regular-season winners.

Koffenberger averaged a career-high 15 points per game as a senior in 1947 and was named a Helms Foundation All-America player. But Duke failed to repeat its tournament success and finished 19-8.

As soon as basketball ended, Koffenberger traded his sneakers for a lacrosse stick.

He had never played lacrosse before college. But he was a quick learner, good enough to be named honorable mention All-America and play in the postseason East-West All-Star game.

"It wasn't that tough making the switch to lacrosse," he recalled. "Many of the concepts were similar to other sports I had played. It was more physical than basketball and required much better conditioning than football. You ran all the time. I fell in love with the game."

By the time Koffenberger graduated, World War II was long over. He turned down a chance to play professional basketball and had a 42-year career as an engineer with Dupont.

He died in 2014 at the age of 88.

13. Duke defeated Virginia 136-72 in 1965, with Jack Marin leading Duke with 25 points.

This was well before a shot clock or a 3-point shot. But the run-and-gun Blue Devils averaged 92.4 points per game that season, the most in school history.

Sophomore Bob Verga led that 1965 team with 21.4 points per game. Marin (19.1), Steve Vacendak (16.2) and Hack Tison (12.0) also made large contributions on the scoreboard.

Duke led Virginia 64-29 at intermission and added to the margin with 72 second-half points. The 64-point victory margin is the largest by Duke against an ACC opponent.

Duke hit 55 of 93 shots from the field (59.1 percent) and 26 for 31 (83.9 percent) from the foul line, while outrebounding Virginia 57-28.

If that sounds like running up the score, Vic Bubas emptied his bench with eight minutes left and Duke up 111-50. Duke used 14 players, including walk-on Burton Fitts, who scored the only two points of his career that night.

This was one of nine times the 1965 team hit the 100-points mark.

The closest Duke has come since was a 130-54 thumping of Harvard in the 1989-90 season.

14. Duke, in 1967. That was 29 years after the first NIT and 13 years after the ACC was founded.

What was the problem?

There were two, actually. The ACC thought that allowing a second ACC team to play in the postseason would de-value the lucrative ACC Tournament, which determined the league's automatic bid to the NCAA Tournament.

But more importantly, the NIT was held in New York City, home of the gamblers who precipitated several point-shaving scandals.

Duke coach Vic Bubas and South Carolina coach Frank McGuire—a New York City native—lobbied the ACC and finally got their way.

In December 1966 the league voted to allow only the tournament runner-up to accept an NIT bid, if offered.

Groundbreaking as it may have been, the ACC's initial foray into the NIT was brief and inauspicious. The 1967 NIT consisted of 14 teams. The NIT gave the ACC representative a first-round bye, but that meant Duke opened on Monday, March 13—two days after the conclusion of the ACC Tournament—in what was the Blue Devils' fourth game in five days.

This wasn't one of Vic Bubas's best teams. Duke started 3-4 but finished the regular season on an 11-2 run, almost entirely on the shoulders of senior Bob Verga, a spectacular long-range shooter. Verga did much of his best work on the road, contributing 23 points in an overtime win at Maryland, 27 at Virginia, 28 at NC State, and 39 at Wake Forest.

But Dean Smith's first Final Four team handled Duke 83-73 in the ACC Tournament title game, despite Verga's 20 points.

An exhausted Duke team fell to the eventual champions, Southern Illinois, which was led by their star Walt Frazier, by a score of 72-63. SIU went on to win the NIT title.

Verga led everyone with 24 points and ended the season averaging 26.1 points per game, a school record that lasted until broken by J.J. Redick in 2006. Had there been a 3-point shot in 1967, Verga would likely have challenged the 30-point-per-game threshold.

Verga averaged 22 points per game at Duke, trailing only Art Heyman and Dick Groat.

15. Bob Gantt played for the Washington Capitols in 1946-47. The Capitols were members of the Basketball Association of America, which became the NBA in 1949 after absorbing a rival circuit, the National Basketball League.

The 6-foot-4, 205-pound Gantt was a solid basketball player for Duke but was best known as an All-America lineman for the Duke football team.

Gantt was a Durham native and was one of four Durham High School products who played for Duke during World War II, graduates of a prep program that gained national attention by winning 70 games in a row. Like Gantt, Gordon Carver was a football/basketball star. Brothers Cedric and Garland Loftis rounded out the quartet.

Gantt was an end on the gridiron and was the first Blue Devil to be named All-America twice. He was on the cover of *Look* magazine in 1942, touted as "Dixie's Finest Athlete." He also won the Southern Conference championship in the shot-put and discus.

The burly Gantt was a post player on the hardcourt and averaged 10 points per game as a sophomore in 1943. His college career later ended after five games as a senior, when he began a military career. He averaged 7.9 points in 51 games at Duke.

Gantt played 23 games for the Capitols, averaging just over three points per game.

Gantt was an NBA footnote, but his descendants were not. Through the 2015-16 season, 66 former Duke Blue Devils have played in the NBA.

16. Bill Werber was voted to the 10-man All-America team by the Christy Walsh Syndicate in 1930. Werber went on to have a standout career as a major league third baseman.

Werber was a fiercely competitive 5-foot-10 athlete from Berwyn, Maryland. He came to Duke at a pivotal time for Duke athletics, around the time Duke joined the Southern Conference and hired Eddie Cameron as the head basketball coach. At that point, the school was still transitioning from Trinity College to Duke University and was undergoing a massive construction project.

Werber would later write of his critical first impressions of Duke.

"I was expecting to find a tranquil green oasis, magnolia trees, and ivy walls. Instead, Duke was a mess. . . . Dust was everywhere. When it rained, mud was six inches deep."

Werber played guard for George Buckheit's last Duke team and Cameron's first two basketball teams and shortstop for Jack Coombs's baseball team. The New York Yankees paid his way through Duke with the understanding that he would join them following his graduation (this was legal in those days).

Werber and classmate Harry Councilor were the keys to Duke's first great Southern Conference team, a 1930 squad that finished 18-2, losing in the Southern Conference Tournament championship game to Alabama.

Cameron called Werber the "best player I ever had. If anything ever opened up between him and the basket, he'd drive like anything for it, knowing he'd either get fouled or score."

Werber went to the big leagues but didn't spend much time with the Yankees. They sent him to the minors after four games and traded him to the Boston Red Sox in 1933.

He hit his stride in Boston, leading the American League in stolen bases in 1934 and 1935 and tying for the lead in 1937, as a member of the Philadelphia Athletics.

Playing for Cincinnati, Werber led off an otherwise uneventful game at Brooklyn on August 26, 1939, thus becoming the first player to bat in a televised game; the broadcast was part of the World's Fair.

He reached the World Series twice for Cincinnati, losing to the Yankees in 1939 but batting .370 (10-27) the following season as Cincinnati defeated Detroit in seven games.

Werber ended his major-league career in 1942, with a .271 career batting average and 215 stolen bases.

He died in 2009 at the age of 100. He was the last living teammate of Babe Ruth.

17. Duke has played four triple-overtime games. Three were ACC games, two were at Duke, and all were played before shot clocks, which means lots of late-game delay offenses.

The first took place in 1958, in Charlottesville, Virginia. Duke trailed 58-54 with three minutes left before forcing a series of turnovers and taking a 60-58 lead.

Virginia tied it with 1:58 left. Duke held for the last shot but Bob Vernon missed.

The teams scored four points each during the first two overtimes, before Virginia got a four-point lead in the third overtime and held on for a 70-68 win.

The loss ended an 11-game Duke winning streak.

Vic Bubas's first Duke team met Dayton for a third-place battle in the 1959 Dixie Classic. The game featured 25 lead changes and 10 ties.

It was 52-52, with seven minutes left, when the teams started holding the ball. Four total points were scored over the course of the last seven minutes of regulation.

Duke scored the first six points of the first overtime but couldn't hold on and ran out of gas in the third overtime, losing 71-63.

Duke's Howard Hurt played all 55 minutes, still a school record.

The most compelling of the triple-overtime games took place on March 2, 1968, at home, against North Carolina. The Tar Heels arrived with a 22-2 record, ranked third in the AP poll.

Duke was ranked tenth, at 19-4.

Both teams were led by senior All-America players, North Carolina forward Larry Miller and Duke center Mike Lewis.

It was Lewis's final home game.

But North Carolina had another star, sophomore wing Charlie Scott, while Lewis was surrounded by complementary players.

One of those was Joe Kennedy, a senior forward. Bubas gave Kennedy the assignment of controlling Miller, and Kennedy was more than up to the task.

Larry Miller was the 1967 and 1968 ACC Player of the Year and averaged over 22 points per game in 1968.

Here's how Kennedy said Duke defended Miller: "Miller was real strong underneath and had the ability to get to the line. You try to keep him from getting the ball and you try to keep him away from the basket and keep him on the perimeter, which was where we wanted him."

Miller would hit only five of 18 from the field on the way to a 15-point game.

But Carolina had other resources, including Scott and junior starters Dick Grubar, Rusty Clark, and Bill Bunting.

North Carolina led 39-37 at intermission and extended the lead to 59-51 at the midpoint of the second half. Lewis was on the bench, having committed four fouls.

An unlikely hero arose. Fred Lind was a 6-foot-8 junior, who went into the game with 21 career points.

He was buried about as far down the bench as a recruited player can be buried.

"Sometimes I would have some good practices," he said, years later. "But I was up and down. I was inconsistent. It was mental concentration. If I was not fired up, then I could be pretty lousy."

Lind concentrated. He converted a three-point play to make the score 59-54. Miller missed a pair of 20-footers at 62-56 and Duke closed to 62-60, with just over six minutes remaining.

The Tar Heels led 64-62, with 4:51 left, when North Carolina coach Dean Smith called for his four corners.

Lewis fouled out shortly after, with 18 points and 18 rebounds.

Lind tied the game with two foul shots, with a minute left. UNC missed two shots in the final seconds.

North Carolina led 69-65 and 71-67 in overtime. But Tony Barone—another deep reserve—hit two foul shots and Lind hit a 22-footer at the buzzer, sending the game into a second overtime.

UNC again jumped on top. But Steve Vandenberg tied the game at 79. North Carolina held the ball for the final 2:25 but Rusty Clark missed at the buzzer.

Overtime number three.

"You're almost oblivious at that stage," Kennedy said. "You're so focused on what's happening, you don't even hear the crowd. It's really one action at a time."

Carolina continued to run the four corners. Leading 82-81, with 1:45 left, Clark moved for the basket. Lind blocked his layup and followed with a left-handed layup over Clark's outstretched hands.

Duke led 83-82, with 1:18 left, its first lead in any of the extra periods. The Blue Devils got a stop and Kennedy hit a pair of foul shots.

Duke led by three. But Grubar hit a jumper and Barone fouled out on a charge, the fourth Blue Devil to be disqualified.

Miller got the ball but Kennedy hounded him into a bad pass out of bounds. Duke beat the pressure and Vandenberg hit a layup.

Clark scored a meaningless layup at the buzzer, leaving Duke with an extraordinary 87-86 victory.

Each team put five players in double figures in scoring, but Lind's 16 points and nine rebounds were the eye-openers.

"It was my biggest game," Lind, who became a public defender in Greensboro, told me years later. "No doubt. But it was just a ball game when you get right down to it. What I do now is more important. But it is one game that I'll always remember."

Duke was no longer a national power when they hosted Clemson on February 24, 1982. This was Mike Krzyzewski's second and worst Duke team.

Senior Vince Taylor (20.3) and junior Chip Engelland (15.2) were the only two Blue Devils to score in double figures in 1982, nobody averaged as many as three assists per game, and the 6-foot-5 Taylor led Duke with 4.9 rebounds per game, the lowest average to lead Duke in rebounding since that statistic started being recorded in 1952.

Duke entered the game with a 9-15 record. Clemson wasn't much better.

It was Taylor's final home game. Duke's second McDonald's All-American, Taylor had started for Duke's 1980 Elite Eight team and led the ACC in scoring in 1982.

He had the best game of his career.

Clemson led 39-32 at the half, but Duke tied the game 62-62 at the end of regulation, 64-64 after one overtime, and 66-66 after two overtimes.

Taylor scored Duke's only two points in the second overtime and blocked a Mike Eppley layup with five seconds left to send the game to a third extra period.

Taylor scored six points in that third overtime. His 15-foot jumper put Duke up 73-72, with 27 seconds left. Clemson held for the final shot, but Taylor forced a turnover and Duke came out victorious.

Taylor ended with a career-high 35 points, in 51 minutes.

"I kept thinking that I should be tired," he said later, "but I wasn't. The adrenaline just carried me. I felt like I could have played forever."

18. Claudius Barrett Claiborne. C.B. Claiborne came to Duke from nearby Danville, Virginia in the fall of 1965, only two years after Duke began admitting African American undergraduates.

The ACC had just begun to integrate its playing fields. Not surprisingly, the league's northernmost outpost, the University of Maryland, was at the forefront of integrating revenue sports. Darryl Hill played wide receiver for the Maryland football team in 1963, breaking the color barrier in that sport.

Maryland followed by signing Billy Jones and Pete Johnson. Both played on Maryland's 1964-65 freshman team, but Johnson was academically ineligible as a sophomore in 1966, making Jones the ACC's first black varsity basketball player.

Claiborne was a superb student-athlete at John Langston High School. He was all set to go to North Carolina A&T when a Duke supporter in the Danville area put Duke and Claiborne together and Claiborne decided to attend Duke on an academic scholarship.

He was the first African American to play basketball at any ACC school other than Maryland.

Claiborne played sparingly as a sophomore and junior, hampered by a bad knee. He did get a rare start as a sophomore against Penn State, in a game where much of the team was suspended for curfew violations. He scored 13 points, as Duke won 89-84.

Claiborne made the rotation as a senior, averaging 6.3 points per game. He scored 49 points in Duke's first four games but gradually lost playing time to younger players. One account cites a dispute with Bubas over Claiborne's Afro. Claiborne scored a career-high 15 points in a 96-70 win over Clemson.

Claiborne endured racial harassment on the road and was unable to attend the team banquet as a freshman, as it was held at a whites-only country club. Claiborne was an activist as a student and missed one game as a senior during a protest.

He graduated with a degree in engineering and later earned a doctorate in marketing from Virginia Tech. Claiborne became a college professor, including a long stint at Texas Southern University.

By the time Claiborne was a senior, Duke had its first recruited African American, forward Don Blackman. Blackman played through his sophomore season at Duke before transferring to Rhode Island. Willie Hodge graduated in 1976, Duke's first four-year African American player.

The modest Claiborne told author Barry Jacobs, "My experiences at Duke were just what you would have expected them to be given that place, given that time. . . . For whatever value or benefit it has . . . that first step was necessary."

19. Sophomore Bernie Janicki averaged 15.9 rebounds per game in 1952. Janicki set the school record for a single game that season, grabbing 31 against North Carolina on Leap Day, February 29.

Janicki was 6-foot-3, not especially big for a center, even in 1952.

But he loved to rebound.

"It was just desire," he explained. "I thought every rebound was mine. If no one was in the way, I went for the ball. If someone was in the way, I went around them or through them."

It helped that he played for a team that shot the ball often. That 1952 Duke team averaged almost 80 field goal attempts per game and made 38 percent of them. Opponents made less than a third of their field goal attempts. The Blue Devils grabbed 58.6 rebounds per game, which also is a school record by a wide margin.

Duke ended its 1952 regular season at home against North Carolina. Dick Groat set a school-record 48 points in that game, the same game Janicki grabbed 31 rebounds.

Janicki never reached those heights again. But he averaged 10.5 rebounds per game as a junior and 6.5 as a senior, when he was sharing rebounds with All-ACC forward Ronnie Mayer.

He ended his Duke career with averages of 15 points and 11.1 rebounds per game, the latter still the fourth-best in school history. He subsequently flew combat missions in Vietnam and retired from the Air Force as a lieutenant colonel.

20. Harold Bradley, in 1955, his fifth season at Duke. Duke lost that game to Villanova by a point and didn't get back to the tournament until 1960.

By many metrics, Bradley was one of the best coaches in ACC history. He compiled a 165-78 mark in nine seasons at Duke, while his ACC .700 winning percentage (56-24) ranks fifth in conference history. He won 102 games in his first five seasons at Duke (only Vic Bubas has more), defeated archrival North Carolina eight straight times, and never had a losing season.

But Bradley's teams never won a Southern Conference or ACC Tournament title at a time when tournament play trumped all.

The affable Bradley was a graduate of Hartwick College in upstate New York. Bradley coached his alma mater for three seasons.

He came to Duke just before the 1950-51 season as terminal cancer forced Duke coach Gerry Gerard to step down.

Aided immeasurably by the presence of Dick Groat, Bradley coached Duke to 20-13 and 24-6 records in his first two seasons.

Bradley coached a fan-pleasing, fast-break offense. On December 15, 1951, Duke beat VMI 102-45, the first time any Duke team passed the 100-points mark.

But what Bradley couldn't do was beat North Carolina State and Everett Case. Groat led Duke to the championship game of the Southern Conference in both 1951 and 1952 and Duke lost both games to State 67-63 and 77-68.

Duke finished first in the 1954 ACC regular season at 9-1, including two wins over State, and got as high as No. 8 in the AP poll, the first Duke team to crack the top 10.

Duke and State met in the semifinals of the ACC Tournament and State prevailed 79-75, ending Duke's season at 21-6.

Duke had another top team in 1955. Senior forward Ronnie Mayer averaged almost 22 points and 12 rebounds per game on the way to earning first-team All-ACC honors.

Bradley's fast-paced attack produced a 115-54 win over Clemson, a 107-75 win over Davidson and 109-89 and 106-92 victories over Virginia.

That team went 11-3 in the ACC, with two of those losses to NC State.

State entered the ACC Tournament as the top seed, with Duke seeded second.

But State was on probation for recruiting violations and could not go to the NCAAs. If they won the tournament, the automatic bid would go to the runner-up.

And Duke was in the opposite bracket from State, meaning their nemesis couldn't knock them out prior to the title game.

The first two rounds played according to seed, with Duke knocking off South Carolina and Virginia—in overtime—while NC State won twice.

Thus, Duke was guaranteed the ACC's automatic bid to the NCAA Tournament regardless of the results of the final game.

Duke led 47-43 at intermission. But perhaps worn down by their overtime effort the night before, Duke shot only

21 percent following intermission and Ronnie Shavlik dominated inside.

State won 87-77. And stayed home.

Having played three games in three days, the exhausted Blue Devils had little time to recover. The East Regional opened on Tuesday night, three days after the ACC title game, in Madison Square Garden.

Duke was matched against Villanova, in the middle game of a triple-header.

The teams knew little about each other. "I believe we can beat Villanova," Bradley told the media, "although I haven't seen the team play. It's tough to prepare for a team you've never seen play."

Duke's shooting woes continued in the first half against the Wildcats, if 21 percent shooting can be dignified as "woes."

Duke actually led 20-19 before falling behind 39-29 at intermission.

Villanova extended the lead to 57-44, with about 10 minutes left. The chances for victory dimmed even more when Mayer fouled out, with four minutes left, having scored only four points, and Duke trailing 69-57.

A free throw extended the lead to 13.

Amazingly, Duke fought back, led by reserve guard Don Tobin. Duke went on a 10-0 run, making it 70-67 with two minutes remaining.

Villanova's Bob Schaefer hit four foul shots and the Blue Devils trailed 74-71, when Duke's Bob Lakata was fouled with 10 seconds left.

The plan was to make the first foul shot, miss the second, and fight for the rebound.

But Lakata missed both. Duke's Junior Morgan scored on the rebound. Villanova in-bounded successfully and ran out the clock on a 74-73 victory.

How to explain the slow start?

Decades later Mayer cited fatigue. "After three games in three days in the ACC Tournament, we were tired. Nothing worked. We weren't ready. We weren't intimidated by Madison Square Garden. In fact, we were disappointed. The Garden wasn't a special place. I thought it was a pit. After playing for the ACC title in front of 12,000 rabid State fans in Reynolds Coliseum, we weren't scared of Madison Square Garden."

Bradley never had another chance at an NCAA win at Duke. His last best chance was in 1958, when an all-senior starting lineup went 11-3 in the ACC and jumped as high as sixth in the AP poll.

But the top-seeded Blue Devils were stunned by Maryland in the ACC Tournament semifinals 71-65, to finish 18-7.

Shortly after the end of the 1959 season, he announced he was leaving Duke for Texas.

Why would any basketball coach leave Duke for Texas?

Texas was a football school, in a football state. But those football revenues enabled them to pay Bradley the princely sum of $12,000 per year, much more than Duke was paying. And he didn't have to recruit against the large, state-supported behemoths; Texas was the large, state-supported behemoth.

It worked out well for all concerned. Duke replaced Bradley with Vic Bubas, who won the tournaments Bradley couldn't win.

But Bradley went 125-73 in eight seasons at Texas, with two NCAA appearances. He won two NCAA Tournament games in 1963, one a consolation game.

Bradley, who died in 1985, ended his career with a 290-151 record in 17 seasons with Duke and Texas. He never did have a losing campaign.

21. Duke's Greg Koubek played in the 1988, 1989, 1990, and 1991 Final Fours. The 6-foot-6 forward started in the 1991 Final Four for Duke's first national title team.

Koubek was from Clifton Park, New York. A McDonald's All-American, Koubek never became a star at Duke but was a solid contributor for four seasons, averaging five points and half that many rebounds over 147 games.

Koubek scored eight points in four East Region wins and then scored eight points in 16 minutes, as Duke lost to Kansas 66-59 in the 1988 Final Four.

Duke again made the national semifinals in Koubek's sophomore season. Koubek went scoreless in 18 minutes in a loss to Seton Hall and scored five points for the tournament.

Duke made it to the title game in 1990, getting blown out by UNLV. Koubek scored two points in both the semifinal win over Arkansas and the loss to Vegas, and eight points overall during the entire tournament.

Koubek played so little early in the 1991 season that he contemplated dropping the sport. After a heart-to-heart with Mike Krzyzewski, Koubek re-dedicated himself to the game and earned a starting spot down the stretch.

Koubek started all six of Duke's NCAA Tournament games that season, scoring 18 points in an 81-67 win over Connecticut and seven points in the 78-61 win over St. John's that sent Duke to the Final Four and a rematch with UNLV.

Duke started a small lineup that tournament, with 6-foot-11 Christian Laettner the only true post player. Krzyzewski put Koubek on Larry Johnson, UNLV's 6-foot-7-250-pound National Player of the Year.

Duke gambled that UNLV center George Ackles couldn't hurt them and used Laettner to double-team Johnson whenever possible.

"The basic principle of man-to-man defense is see the ball, see your man," Koubek said. "K told me to forget the ball. Get in front of Johnson and make them throw it over the top, where Christian would double him. It was constant battling. But we never let them get into a rhythm."

Koubek only scored two points but helped hold Johnson to 13 points, barely half his season average.

And Duke pulled off the upset. The Blue Devils played Kansas two nights later for the championship.

Koubek wasn't Duke's best player; far from it. But he was the only senior in the rotation, and his word carried weight.

"We remembered what happened the year before, when we never really came down from the [semifinal] win over Arkansas," he told his teammates. "Beating UNLV would have made most teams' season. But it didn't make ours. Second place wasn't good enough."

Koubek not only started the title game but scored the game's first five points, giving Duke a lead it never relinquished.

Those were his only points of the game.

Koubek came to Duke with two other players. Joe Cook flunked out after his junior season. Injury-plagued center Clay Buckley stayed for four seasons but did not play in either the 1988 or 1991 Final Fours.

22. Vic Bubas suspended nine players for missing curfew, including four starters. Bob Verga was the only starter left. Yet,

Verga and some guys no one had ever heard of defeated Penn State on January 3, 1967 by a score of 89-84.

This all came about after Duke had defeated Wake Forest in Greensboro on December 30, 1966. Much of the team had celebrated the victory and got back much too late for Bubas's liking.

Mike Lewis, one of the culprits, said, "We were stupid and got caught."

Verga, who wasn't out with his teammates after the Wake Forest game, was joined in the starting lineup by four deep reserves, none of whom had ever started a varsity game at Duke. The only reserve was a practice player.

Amazingly, Duke won. Verga, who played the entire game, was the primary reason, hitting 16 of 31 from the field and six for eight from the line, for a game-high 38 points. Sophomores Steve Vandenberg and C.B. Claiborne added 16 and 13 points respectively, with Vandenberg pulling down 14 rebounds.

23. Three, by three different players, all ranked among the Duke greats. All three came in Duke wins.

Art Heyman was the first. Assists weren't an official statistic in 1963, but the ACC decided to experiment that year in the tournament and Heyman was credited with a 21-point, 18-rebound, 10-assist game against Virginia.

Duke won the game 89-70.

Freshman forward Gene Banks had the second, in 1978. He scored 13 points, with 12 rebounds and 11 assists in a 105-63 defeat of overmatched Lehigh.

Shelden Williams had the only triple-double involving blocks. Williams had 11 boards and 10 rejections, to go along with 19 points as Duke defeated Maryland 76-52 in 2006.

Duke has had some tantalizing near-misses as well. Kenny Dennard had 11 steals in a 1979 game against Maryland, Duke's only double-digit steals performance. Dennard added 13 points but only five rebounds.

Duke won that game 87-78.

The most curious near-miss came in the 1994 ACC Tournament. Points is the easiest triple-double category to reach. But Duke's Cherokee Parks could muster only eight, to go along with 10 rebounds and 10 blocked shots in a 77-64 win over Clemson.

Thomas Hill against California in the 1993 NCAA Tournament. Cal won 82-77, ending Duke's 13-game NCAA-Tournament winning streak. (AP Photo/Fred Jewell)

24. Thomas Hill won a bronze medal in the 110-meter high hurdles at the 1972 (Munich) Olympics. His son, Thomas II, scored 1,594 points in four seasons at Duke (1989–1993).

Thomas came to Duke in the same class as Bobby Hurley and Billy McCaffrey. A 6-foot-5 lefty, he arrived as an athletic defender and rebounder but developed into a deadly scorer.

Hill averaged over 11 points per game for Duke's 1991 NCAA champions, and his 14.6 points per game made him the second-leading scorer on the 1992 title team. He averaged a career-best 15.7 points per game as a senior in 1993.

Teammate Greg Koubek calls Hill "the unsung hero" of those championship teams. "He would do anything to help the team win, sacrifice his body, get on the floor for a loose ball, hit a big shot."

25. Duke and South Carolina were engaged in a nasty and complicated dispute over a player named Mike Grosso, a highly-touted 6-foot-9 recruit from New Jersey. Like many prepsters from Greater New York, Grosso elected to cast his lot with Frank McGuire, who was head coach at South Carolina.

The ACC had an 800 SAT minimum in those days. Grosso missed.

But the limit was only for scholarships. Grosso attended South Carolina anyway, his tuition supposedly paid for by an uncle. The ACC investigated and determined that South Carolina was funding his enrollment.

Grosso had played on the South Carolina freshman team but was ruled ineligible by the ACC before his sophomore season.

He transferred to Louisville.

McGuire and Duke AD Eddie Cameron didn't much care for each other and McGuire was critical of Cameron even before the Grosso controversy, complaining, "These officials are scared to death of Cameron. He's the one who runs this conference."

McGuire claimed that Cameron—and to a lesser extent, UNC AD Chuck Erickson—blew the whistle on his program and asserted "I have never gotten in the gutter with the skunks before but this time I have."

The rhetoric became so heated that the ACC gave Duke and South Carolina the option of not playing their regular season games against one another, in the interest of safety.

Duke accepted the offer. "We are not mad," Cameron said at the time, "but it is the feeling of the Duke administration that this incident has grown out of proportion and a cooling off period is desirable."

Thus Duke and South Carolina played 12 ACC games in 1967, while the other six ACC teams played 14.

As fate would have it, they met in the ACC Tournament. Duke won 69-66, without incident.

26. Duke's 2002 team. Jason Williams, Mike Dunleavy Jr., and Carlos Boozer were the trio. All were juniors that season and all left for the NBA following the season. Williams won all the National Player of the Year awards, Dunleavy was consensus second-team All-America, and Boozer was third-team.

Williams, Dunleavy, and Boozer arrived at Duke for the 1999-2000 season, replenishing the Blue Devils after the post-1999 talent exodus that included Elton Brand and Trajan Langdon.

All three started for Duke's 2001 title team and hoped to repeat, with sophomore Chris Duhon also returning and transfer forward Dahntay Jones and freshman wing Daniel Ewing replacing graduated starters Shane Battier and Nate James.

For much of the season, a repeat seemed like a realistic possibility. The 6-foot-2 Williams (21.3), 6-foot-9 Dunleavy (17.3) and 6-foot-9 Boozer (18.2) combined for 56.8 points per game, with Boozer and Dunleavy combining for 16 rebounds per game.

Duke began and ended the season ranked No. 1 in the AP poll, started 23-1, and captured the ACC Tournament with wins by 12, 15, and 30 points.

(left to right) Daniel Ewing, Mike Dunleavy, Jason Williams, Dahntay Jones, and Carlos Boozer celebrate Duke's 2002 ACC Tournament championship. (AP Photo/Bob Jordan)

But the season ended at 31-4 in the Sweet Sixteen, where a scrappy Indiana team overcame a big deficit to edge Duke 74-73.

One ACC team has since duplicated the feat. North Carolina placed Tyler Zeller, John Henson, and Harrison Barnes on the 2012 All-ACC first team.

27. He beat the Heels. West only scored 142 points at Duke. But when he met his moment, he was ready.

The moment was January 22, 1972, the end of a tie game between Duke and North Carolina. It had not been a typical

Duke-Carolina game. At halftime, Duke renamed Duke Indoor Stadium Cameron Indoor Stadium, after retiring AD Eddie Cameron.

West wasn't the guy you would expect to have the game in his hands. A 6-foot-2 guard, he had scored only 16 total points in his first two seasons.

But graduation and transfers had left Duke without a lot of options.

North Carolina had options—six future pro players' worth. The 7-6 Blue Devils were overmatched against the 12-1 Tar Heels.

But we all know what they say about rivalry games.

Center Alan Shaw and Duke's 2-3 zone held Robert McAdoo to one for 12 shooting. Gary Melchionni shredded North Carolina's press and forwards Richie O'Connor and Chris Redding combined for 48 points.

Duke had the ball with eight seconds left, 74-74.

"We thought the pressure would be enormous on Melchionni and we didn't think we could get the ball inside," Waters said later. "Robby was a senior, he was careful with the ball, and he could shoot. We went with a hunch."

"They [the coaches] knew I could hit that shot," West said. "That side of the court was my sweet spot. When you're a shooter and the ball leaves your fingers right, you know it."

It was about 18 feet, just left of the center circle, and nothing but net.

It wasn't a true buzzer-beater. North Carolina had three seconds left and even got off a desperation heave by Dennis Wuycik.

But it never came close. Cameron's first game as Cameron ended with the students rushing the court.

Waters calls this the biggest win of his four-year tenure as Duke's head coach. "A loss would have been an injustice," he said. "A lot of things had to fall in place. We got a tremendous response from our kids."

28. Mike Gminski won the 11-year-old age group in 1971, in Los Angeles. Less than a decade later, he was one of the nation's best college basketball players.

Gminski never actually played organized football. Already six feet tall, 170 pounds by age 11, Gminski was always too big for his age group.

Football's loss was basketball's gain. He put his size to better use on the basketball court, averaging 40 points per game for Masuk High in Monroe, Connecticut in 1976.

Gminski also was a superb student, good enough to graduate from high school a year early.

Duke got a break when Blue Devils player Terry Chili worked a summer camp at the University of Maryland attended by Gminski, who alerted Chili of his plans.

Other schools—including North Carolina—recruited Gminski, but Bill Foster leveraged his head start into a commitment.

"It was a great fit on every level," Gminski said later. "Great academics, a beautiful campus, lots of students from the northeast. Plus, I was looking for a place where I could play right away."

Gminski was 6-foot-11, 250 pounds when he showed up at Duke. He turned 17 just weeks before beginning his freshman season.

Despite his youth, he made an immediate impact. Gminski's first college game was against Wake Forest, in the Big Four Tournament. He grabbed eight rebounds in that game and 14 in the next, a consolation win over NC State. Gminski shot 10 for 10 in his third game, against Johns Hopkins, and never looked back. He out-rebounded Washington's senior center James Edwards in his fourth game at Duke and Edwards went on to play 19 years in the NBA.

There was no 3-point shot in those days, and Gminski's range didn't extend that far anyway. But inside 15 feet he was an accurate and versatile shooter, scoring on jumpers, put-backs, layups, and a devastating jump hook. He made almost 80 percent of his foul shots at Duke.

Gminski also mastered the art of blocking shots without getting into foul trouble. Playing mostly in a zone, he had 345 blocks in 122 games at Duke, against only 240 fouls. Gminski never fouled out of a game at Duke.

In a 1978 NCAA Tournament game against the University of Pennsylvania, Gminski sparked a late 14-2 run by blocking shots on three consecutive possessions.

Duke won 84-80.

His number 43 was retired right before his final home game, against Clemson. He was the first Duke player to have a jersey retired since Dick Groat in 1952.

No one bothered to tell Gminski that his number was being retired. "It was a complete surprise. It had been so long since Groat, it didn't even occur to me. I was already a wreck because of senior day and then this."

He got past the shock of it all in time to score 29 points, grab 19 rebounds ,and block seven shots to lead Duke to an overtime win.

Plagued by injuries and rumors of Foster's impending move to South Carolina, Duke struggled to a 7-7 ACC mark. But the Blue Devils rallied for an ACC Tournament title. Gminski tallied 59 points and 34 rebounds in three games, as well as the game-winning points in a 73-72 win over Maryland in the title game.

Duke advanced to the NCAAs, where the Blue Devils opened by defeating a slow-down Pennsylvania effort, 52-42. Gminski scored 19 points, the only player on either team to score in double figures.

Next was Kentucky, at Rupp Arena. Gminski led Duke with 17 points and seven rebounds and fouled out Kentucky star center Sam Bowie in nine minutes.

Duke won 55-54.

The Midwest title game matched Gminski and Duke against Purdue and their 7-foot-2 center Joe Barry Carroll, the only college center rated higher than Gminski at that time.

Gminski (17 points, nine rebounds, two blocks) and Carroll (26 points, six rebounds, one block) battled to a draw, but Duke lost starting forwards Gene Banks and Kenny Dennard to fouls and fell 68-60.

Gminski ended his Duke career with 2,323 points, 1242 rebounds, and 345 blocks. He was Duke's career leader in all three categories when he graduated and still ranks fifth, second, and second respectively.

The G-Man was the most honored Duke player of the 1970s. He shared ACC Rookie of the Year accolades with NC State's "Hawkeye" Whitney in 1977 and was then selected first-team All-ACC in 1978, 1979, and 1980. He was named 1979 ACC Player of the Year and was consensus All-America in both 1979 and 1980.

29. Tate Armstrong, at Virginia, in 1977. It was the last game Armstrong would play in a Duke uniform.

Armstrong broke his right wrist in the first half of that game. But he continued playing anyway, leading Duke to an 82-74, overtime win, which broke a five-year ACC road losing streak.

Armstrong went to high school in Houston. His high school coach, Roy Kieval, was a scorekeeper for the Houston Rockets. Through Kieval's efforts, Armstrong got a chance to scrimmage against some Houston players, including former Duke star Jack Marin.

Marin alerted then Duke coach Bucky Waters.

Duke liked what they saw. So did Armstrong.

"The visit was what sewed it up," Armstrong said. "The Duke Chapel, the Gardens, and Cameron Indoor Stadium, all in the spring. It sold me."

Armstrong never played for Waters, who resigned before Armstrong's freshman season (1973-74) and was replaced by assistant coach Neil McGeachy.

The 6-foot-2 Armstrong played center in high school but had to become a college guard. He averaged six points per game off the bench for a 10-16 Duke team.

Bill Foster replaced McGeachy and Armstrong moved into the starting lineup, averaging just under 10 points per game.

The three leading scorers on that 1975 team were seniors. Foster told Armstrong he would need to play major minutes in 1976 and needed to improve his conditioning.

Armstrong went home and ran 15–20 miles every day in the Texas heat.

The result was the second greatest single-season scoring improvement in Duke history. Armstrong scored 42 points against Clemson, 40 against NC State, and 33 in the ACC Tournament against Maryland.

A first team All-ACC player, Armstrong ended the season averaging 24.2 points per game. Only Dick Groat, Art Heyman, Bob Verga, and J.J. Redick have ever averaged more points per game in a Duke season. Despite playing on the perimeter, Armstrong shot over 52 percent from the field.

He also led Duke with four assists per game.

But Duke kept losing, finishing 13-14, 10 of those losses by six points or less.

"I struggled with the fact that I was scoring so much while we were losing," Armstrong said later. "The individual accomplishments were great, but you're judged by how well you do as a team. We talked about it but simply couldn't see a better way for the team to be successful."

Armstrong did have an opportunity to play on a winning squad. He was one of seven ACC players to make the 1976 United States Olympic team. Coached by Dean Smith, that team captured a gold medal.

Armstrong scored 16 points in six games.

Armstrong continued with his heroics as a senior. But Duke started winning some of those close games. Duke went to Knoxville and stunned 15th-ranked Tennessee and their stars Bernard King and Ernie Grunfeld, 81-78. Armstrong scored 29 points. He also hit a buzzer-beater to defeat Washington 83-81 (35 points) and a buzzer-beater to defeat Richmond 65-63. Armstrong's 23 points keyed Duke to an 84-82 win over NC

State in the Big Four, ending a nine-game losing streak to the Wolfpack.

Duke went to Charlottesville on January 17 with a 10-3 record, 0-2 in the ACC, and hoping to break a 27-game ACC road losing streak.

Armstrong dove to the floor, scrambling for a loose ball, early in the game. "I knew right away it was broken," he said years later. "The pain was intense."

Foster and Duke trainer Max Crowder wanted to pull Armstrong from the game at halftime. Armstrong was so adamant in his refusal that he recalls throwing a bucket of ice against a wall. "They were going to have to shoot me to get me off the court."

Duke trailed 35-31 at the half, but Armstrong kept them in it and then more, hitting 14 of 24 from the field.

Armstrong ended the season averaging 22.7 points per game, with an astonishing 55.5 shooting percentage. He would have led the ACC in scoring had he played more games.

Absent Armstrong, Duke's promising season fell apart. Duke moved to 11-3 with the Virginia win but lost 10 of their final 13 to finish 14-13.

Duke's breakthrough season came a year later, but without Armstrong.

Armstrong never played in a postseason game at Duke. But he might have been Duke's best player between Vic Bubas and the 1978 revival.

30. Gerry Gerard replaced Eddie Cameron in 1942 when Cameron took over the head football coaching job. Gerard remained head soccer coach until 1945 but continued as head basketball coach through 1950.

If you're thinking that this had something to do with World War II, you would be correct.

The chain of events started when football coach Wallace Wade joined the Army in 1942. He served as an artillery officer in Europe, rising to the rank of colonel.

Eddie Cameron was head basketball coach at the time but also was an assistant football coach. Cameron dropped basketball and took over the head football position.

Trading basketball for football made sense in 1942, a time when football was the campus apex sport. Duke had just hosted the 1942 Rose Bowl, which was moved from Pasadena after the Japanese attack on Pearl Harbor.

Gerard had been at Duke since 1931. He had been a multi-sport athlete at the University of Illinois, where he was best known for backing up gridiron great Red Grange.

He came to Duke to run the intramural program but started the soccer program in 1935.

World War II totally transformed American college sports. Duke became a naval training school. Most male students were either in the Navy V-12 program or studying to become Methodist ministers.

Players came, players left, and coaches didn't have much of a say in either.

Consider Bob Gantt. A football and basketball star at Duke, Gantt returned to Duke in 1945 as an opponent, a member of the Norfolk Naval Training Station (NNTS) team, which beat Duke 59-37. Football great Otto Graham—who also played basketball at Northwestern—twice played Duke as a member of Carolina Pre-Flight.

Duke played lots of schools like NNTS and Carolina Pre-Flight during World War II, including Fort Bragg, Camp Butner, Norfolk Air Station, Camp Perry, and Cherry Point.

But college teams—many featuring officers in training—provided the bulk of the competition. Duke went 20-6 in 1943 but lost in the Southern Conference Tournament title game to George Washington. The following year Duke took a 10-13 mark into the conference tournament and won the whole thing, finishing 13-13.

Normalcy started returning for the 1945-46 season, which was perhaps Gerard's best team. Led by Ed Koffenberger, Duke finished second in the Southern Conference at 12-2, trailing 13-1 North Carolina; Duke and Carolina split two games.

Wake Forest upset North Carolina in the ACC Tournament and Duke handled the Deacons 49-30 in the championship game, Duke's fifth Southern Conference title in nine seasons.

The NCAA snubbed Duke, picking North Carolina as the southeastern representative to the NCAA Tournament. The Tar Heels finished second, while Duke ended its season at 21-6.

Everett Case arrived at NC State the following season and Duke wouldn't win another conference tournament until 1960.

Duke was still competitive, finishing 19-8, 17-12, and 13-9 under Gerard.

But all wasn't well with Gerard, who became ill at a tournament in the summer of 1949. Diagnosed with cancer, he was given six months to live.

Gerard didn't have an assistant coach and Duke wanted to be prepared for the inevitable. They hired Arnold "Red" Auerbach, who had recently resigned from the head coaching job with the Washington Capitols.

Duke parked Auerbach in the P.E. department, where he worked with emerging star Dick Groat. But Gerard rallied and Auerbach grew increasingly uneasy with the circumstances.

"Gerry had cancer and nobody felt worse about it than me," Auerbach said later. "I didn't want to have to get a job that way."

Auerbach went back to the pros after three months, where he became one of the most successful coaches in NBA history.

What if Auerbach had stayed at Duke? That will remain one of the great what-ifs in Duke basketball history.

Gerard made it through the 1950 season but resigned shortly after the end of the season.

He died January 17, 1951.

31. Bob Bender for Indiana in 1976 and Duke in 1978.

Bender was a *Parade* All-America guard from Illinois. He averaged two points per game as a freshman in 1976 for a title team that remains the last unbeaten team in men's NCAA Division I basketball.

Bender played only a mop-up minute in the title game, an 86-68 win over Michigan.

Bender decided to transfer from Indiana in the fall of 1976. Knight and Duke coach Bill Foster were close. Knight suggested Duke, and Foster and Bender were receptive.

Bender had to sit out the first half of the 1977-78 season at Duke. He made a significant impact once he began to play though, and scored 11 points in a 92-84 win over North Carolina, Duke's first ACC win over the Tar Heels since 1972.

A big scorer in high school, Bender became a playmaker at Duke. He shared the point guard spot with fellow transfer John Harrell (who came from North Carolina Central) as Duke advanced to the 1978 Final Four. Bender played 19 minutes off the bench in a win over Notre Dame and 16 minutes in a loss to Kentucky in the title game, scoring seven points with four assists against Kentucky.

Bender took over as starting point guard in 1979 and 1980. He was third in the ACC with 4.8 assists per game in 1980.

His career-high of 16 points came against NC State in the 1979 ACC Tournament. Hours after Duke's win, Bender suffered a season-ending appendectomy.

He almost made it back to the Final Four in 1980, helping Foster's last Duke team to the Mideast Regional title game. Bender ended his college career with 10 points and three assists in a 68-60 loss to Purdue.

Bender went into coaching, for six seasons as an assistant for Mike Krzyzewski and Duke, then with stints as head coach at Illinois State and Washington. He got Washington into the 1998 Sweet Sixteen, where they lost a close game to Connecticut.

32.

1E
2D
3A
4B
5C

McLeod, Jones, Curry, and Hood all made All-ACC at Duke—Curry twice—and all four play or played in the NBA. Knee problems short-circuited Obi's Duke career.